A Breath Of Fresh Air
Kempo Karate Novice to Intermediate

by
James Moclair

Bloomington, IN  Milton Keynes, UK

AuthorHouse™
1663 Liberty Drive, Suite 200
Bloomington, IN 47403
www.authorhouse.com
Phone: 1-800-839-8640

AuthorHouse™ UK Ltd.
500 Avebury Boulevard
Central Milton Keynes, MK9 2BE
www.authorhouse.co.uk
Phone: 08001974150

©2006 James Moclair. All rights reserved.

No part of this book may be reproduced, stored in a retrieval system, or transmitted by any means without the written permission of the author.

First published by AuthorHouse 7/26/2006

ISBN: 1-4259-3030-1 (e)
ISBN: 1-4259-3029-8 (sc)

Printed in the United States of America
Bloomington, Indiana

This book is printed on acid-free paper.

Table of Contents

Introduction 1

Ready Position 5

Fighting Stance 6

Rising Block And Forward Stance 8

Reverse Outside Forearm Block, Forward Stance 10

Inside Forearm Block, Forward Stance 11

Outside Forearm Block, Forward Stance 12

Downward Sweeping Block, Straddle Stance 13

Lunge Punch, Forward Stance 14

Reverse Punch, Forward Stance 17

Fighting Stance Into Front Jab 19

Front Kick 21

Side Kick 23

Round House Kick 25

Back Kick 27

Kicking With The Top Of Your Foot 29

Front Kick Using The Heel 30

Axe Kick 31

Front Angle Kick 33

Breaking Your Fall 34

Side Breakfall 34

Back Breakfall 35

"To Fight Or Not To Fight, That Is The Question" 36

Defence From A Downward Blow 40

Kiai On The Reverse Punch 43

Side Blow, To The Head 44

Quarter Stepping 47

Straight Punch To The Face 49

Front Strangulation 52

Rear Strangulation 56

Front Bear Hug, Arms Pinned 59

Front Bear Hug, Arms Free 62

v

Rear Bear Hug, Arms Pinned	67
Front Hair Pull	71
Hair Pull, From The Rear	75
Yellow Belt Syllabus	78
Backward roll	78
Forward roll	80
Rising Cross Block And Forward Stance	82
Downward Cross Block And Forward Stance	84
Knife Edge Block Strike And Back Stance	86
Cat Stance And Back Fist Strike	88
Hammer Fist And Forward Stance	90
Palm Heel Strike And Forward Stance	92
Front Kick Front Leg	94
Close Quarter Side Kick	96
Round House Kick Front Leg	98
Turning Back Kick	100
Turning Round House Kick	103
Lapel Hold And Downward Blow	105
Lapel Hold And Side Blow	110
Lapel Hold And Straight Punch To The Face	114
Hands Restrained From The Front	118
Hands Restrained From The Rear	123
Single Lapel Hold	127
Both Lapels Held	131
Pull Back On The Shoulder From The Rear	136
Pull Back On The Shoulder And Side Blow The Face	140
Pull On The Sleeve From The Rear	144
Pull On Wrist From The Rear With A Side Blow	147
The Beginning Of The Orange Belt Syllabus	151
Arc Fist Bock	151
Ridge Hand Strike	153
Elbow Block	154
Upper Cut	155
Round House Punch	156

Wall Fighting Stance	157
Defence Against A Wall	159
Floor Fighting Stance	163
Floor Defence Against A Kick To The Head	164
Floor Defence With The Attacker Doing A Kick To The Ribs	169
Defence From Strangle On The Floor	173
Front Kick Defence	177
Side Kick Defence	181
Round House Kick Defence	186
Turning Back Kick	189
Forearm Nelson Attack	192
How To Do A Forearm Nelson	192
Side Head Lock	199
Back Leg Crescent Kick	203
Front Leg Crescent Kick	205
Jumping Crescent Kick	207
Reverse Jumping Crescent Kick	210
Back Leg Reverse Crescent Kick	212
Front Leg Reverse Crescent Kick	215
Japanese Terminology And Glossary - A through Z	218
Martial Arts Ranks	230
Pre Black Belt Ranks	230
Black Belt Ranks	230
Japanese Numbers 1 through 20	231
Karate Syllabus	232
With Thanks	239
About the Author	241

Introduction

Hi everyone my name is James Moclair. For the last forty years plus I have trained in various martial arts. Since 1980 I have taught professionally and do this seven days a week. The average time I spend training in my Dojo (Club) each week is about 76 hours.

The Karate system that I teach is based on the kempo karate, however over the years I have evolved my own hybrid system. The system is quite unique; it has hard and soft blocks. Strike blocks that are extremely powerful. Step back blocks. Reinforced blocks and rolling hand strikes. Numerous hand and foot techniques and floor kicks. Locks and throws and immobilisation techniques are also employed. Black belts use traditional weapons like Sai dagger: (a steel trident) Kama sickle: (scythe) Tonfa: (wood staff with a handle on the side) Jo staff: (a short staff usually between 49" and 54") Bo staff: (wood staff around five to six feet long) Tanto: (knife) Nunchaku: (two sticks attached by cord or chain.) and Katana, (Japanese long sword) as part of their training and gradings's.

Looking at the white belt syllabus the blocks and kicks are much the same as any other karate system. The difference becomes more apparent with the attacks and defences. As you look further into the system you will notice some radical differences.

My Karate system has no sport in it. I for one believe that sport is killing the martial arts and most clubs now have a very watered down martial sports system that is effective in competition against an similar trained opponent but is quite useless in a real live attack. Remember there are no referee's out in the street; you are on your own.

If you are constantly training to pull your punches or to make light contact or in some cases, no contact then how will you fare in a real fight? You are only as good as the training you put in. Just another thought, what happens if in a fight the attacker grabs you and wrestles you to the floor, how are the martial sports people going to do then? Getting their sporty butts kicked is a reasonable answer.

Another difference is that I do not have sparring in the system, no protection wear is allowed and gum shields are the only optional. To date, not one of my students has even a gum shield. Now, as you get over this little revelation let me explain what we do and the reason why.

We do knock down's. You start in a standing position and fight using hand and foot techniques; if you get close you can throw or sweep your partner and also proceed to grapple on the mat area. Arm locks, wrist locks, strangulation techniques and strikes are allowed from the floor. To submit all you have to do is tap your partner. You would only do this type of fighting from green belt upward. By then you will have a reasonable amount of techniques under you belt.

It all may sound a little rough but it is very safe, we do not have any accidents. The children love this form of fighting, they find it quite natural but above all it is what you will experience in a real fight situation.

You may at this stage think the above is all very well but why not wear protective equipment? Well the answer is simple; if you wear protective gear when you're training you become dependant on it. This will put you at a distinct disadvantage should a real situation occur. Plus you have the problem of gloves and mitts, in the kempo system I have 32 basic hand techniques it is impossible to use these with the restriction of gloves or mitts.

Groin protection is also not used on any of my classes. From a street point of it is number one in the top twenty for someone to attack so my view is that you need to learn to protect this area. You can do this with the correct stances and posture and if all else fails come on to one of my combat Ki (Internal power) classes where I will teach how to take a kick in the groin and various other vulnerable parts of the body without injury.

Kata is set form of techniques and movements that are practiced by on your own. In most karate system's the kata is made up by the senior instructor and then every one who practices that particular style does the same kata. Some karate styles have up to thirty five kata's. I have a different approach; my system has no set kata's. Each student when taking their brown belt has to compose their own thirty two move kata and again when taking their black belt they again compose a new fifty two move kata. Black belts taking going through their Dan grades compose a new kata for each weapon they use.

You may find my approach to kata's a little odd but in my defence I believe that everyone is a unique individual. Some people have better abilities than others, some are more flexible. People come in all shapes and sizes. When a young child first comes to learn karate they often find it difficult to know their right from their left. Their balance is poor and they are uncoordinated. This changes very quickly as do their height and weight, for the rest of their lives the body will constantly change. Kata's too should evolve with changes that we all experience in our bodies. What you can do when you are in your twenties you may not be able to do when you are fifty. Even the martial art that you practise should change to compensate for the ageing process. When one of my student's develops his/her kata it is done under my supervision they have to show that it is practical. As the student gets better at karate they can then add changes and modifications to the kata.

I also believe that your mental attitude is greatly altered by the way that you train. This reminds me of that great saying "Train hard fight easy" "Train easy Fight hard"

P.M.A (Positive Mental Attitude.) If you believe that you can achieve something then the only thing that stands in your way is the hard work ahead but in time you will eventually be a winner. However if you think this looks too hard for me then you are a loser. I have always enjoyed a good hard training session. To be good at anything you must work hard at it. It is only through repetition that you will master a martial art. And it is only through having a good positive mental attitude that any goal or ambition in life can be achieved.

Training in a martial arts has numerous benefits, you will get fit, fitness is so important. You cannot expect to be a first class martial artist if your level of fitness is poor. Further to be able to fight in a real situation you will need all the stamina you can muster. Building and feeling confident about yourself is another benefit that comes with the martial arts training. The confidence you will feel will expand into all aspects of your life and that alone is worth a pot of gold. Another big benefit is that training in martial arts calms you down, you can let out your aggressions with a good work out and when you have been training for a while you start to feel relaxed in you view of life. The bonus benefit is, that you will meet some real nice people and make some good friends.

Over the years that I have practiced my martial arts I have seen that the world is far more violent now then when I first started. Muggings, robbery, rape, burglary and car crimes and murder are happening every second of every day and the police are like a dog without teeth. It may sound harsh to say this about the police but see how many of the crimes I have mentioned being solved and the criminals put in jail................

I rest my case.

Everyone has the right to defend themselves, but some martial art system's are to aggressive and you can end up in trouble with the law if while you go over the top in defending yourself. My Kempo Karate takes this into consideration and has cut off point's to allow you to use reasonable force against the would be attacker. My philosophy is that you walk away from a situation if possible. You may even try to talk your way of any conflict. The last resort is to use your martial skills, but if you have use them then, woe behold the attacker or attackers

If you are just starting out in your martial arts career I would like to offer a few tips on what to look for when joining a club. It is very difficult to get the best without shopping around. Look in your yellow pages for the more established clubs or other such directories. You can also go onto the internet and look for clubs that have web sites. Draw up a list of clubs that you think may fit the bill, and then go visit them. Most clubs will welcome you and provide literature on the various classes. Don't be afraid to ask question's, like what grade is the instructor, how long as he/she been doing martial arts and who graded them. Most good quality instructor will be only too pleased to tell you about themselves, because they are proud of their achievements.

I would advise to seek out the highest grade instructor. As far as I am concerned the best instructors are those who are in their mid forties and fifties or over. They are the ones with a wealth of knowledge.

Insurance is also a big issue these day's. Make sure that any club you visit or train has the following insurance. Member to member personal accident insurance, public liability insurance, professional indemnity insurance.

Ask about the price of the classes and membership fees and also grading fees. Also ask about the Gi (Suite) and what price are they. Expect to pay more for a professional full time dojo (Club). The overheads on such places are greater than if someone is running one class a week from a church hall. I would personally seek a professional dojo (Club) as you will have more opportunity to practice and train. Also you will probably find that their is a professional instructor heading the instruction. A person worth his/her weight in gold.

Any club that you look at whether it is a full time dojo or a club that hire's a room should have enough space for the members to train. If the art involves any throws, sweeps or any more that take you to the floor then, I would advise that they should a mat area. If throws are part of the system and no mats are used then leave this club alone. Don't take any rubbish that it toughens you up to fall on a hard floor.

Any club you look at should have a good etiquette and the club; mats should be clean and tidy. If the club smells like a tramps arm pit don't buy a nose clip just leave. Personal hygiene is very important in martial arts.

Before parting with any cash ask if you can sit in and watch a class, this is a reasonable request and it will allow you to see the quality of the instructor in action and also allow you to see the quality of the students. If the students look good then you are on the right track, however if the students look bad head for the hills.

A quick word on the instructor, don't expect a shoalin monk. At best look for someone who, ignoring their age has looked after themselves. Massive beer bellies do not fit the martial arts bill as do instructors who have to nip out for a quick smoke. Smoking and martial arts do not mix well. Drugs are defiantly out. The saying "Practice what you teach" comes into order.

If you find a club that looks great but is the farthest away, be prepared to travel, it will be worth it in the long run.

The above advice is based only on the standards that I have and will always have within my own clubs.

I do not intend in this book to write on history of Kempo Karate, many other authors have done this. This book will concentrate on the basic techniques of the art first and then expand through the more advanced techniques. Basics are the foundation of any martial art; they must be constantly practiced in order to maintain the structure and integrity of the art.

This book is only meant as a guide and not a complete training programme. If you decide to practice any of the technique in this book then I recommend that they are practiced in the safety of a Dojo (club.) Do not try any of the techniques in your home or any other such place. It always ends up with some kind of disaster or accident.

You must start every session with a warm up, do not rush through your warm up. You can easily pull or strain yourself. Pulled or strain muscles takes months to get over and that means missing valuable training sessions. Prevention is better than treatment.

Also remember to cool down at the end of each session.

I have not included any exercises in this book. The reason for this is I would have to write a separate book on exercise as it is quite a complex subject. For example exercises with children are different than exercises with adults.

You cannot do any martial art on an empty stomach, make sure that you eat about three hours before you training session. Also do not eat directly before you train, this is fatal. Well maybe that is a slight bit harsh but I'm sure you get the message.

Fluid intake is very important when you are doing any martial art, I have found over the years that water if by far the best. But it is your choice; there are lots of sport drinks on the market for you to try. Just remember to keep your fluid levels up and do not get dehydrated. Do not drink alcohol before a training session.

Now it is time to start with the basics, even if you have done martial arts before you may find my approach interesting. I will try to break each move down so it is easy to follow.

Ready position is done by standing with your feet together, hands by your sides. As shown in illustration 1, a.

Ready Position

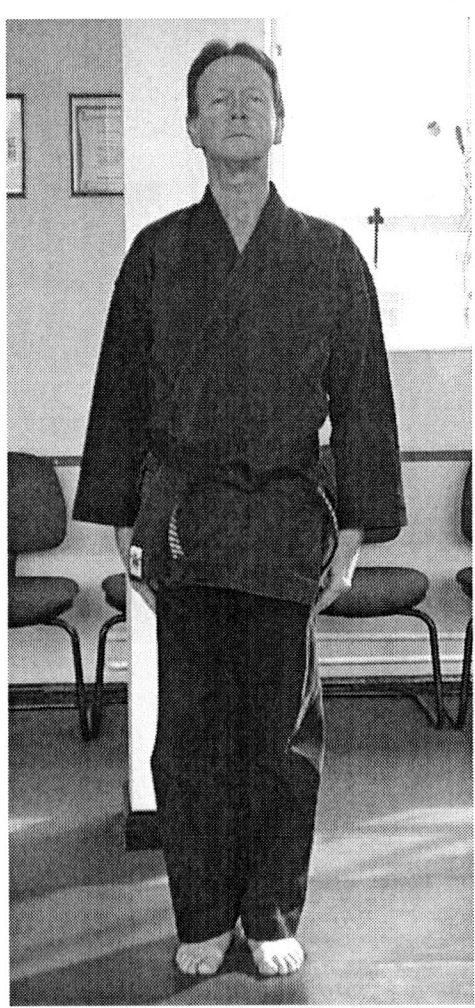 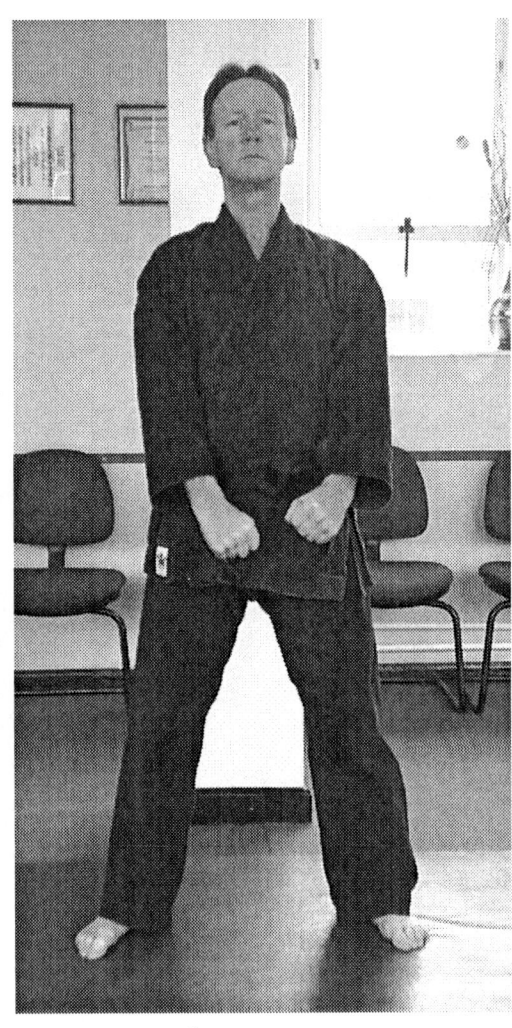

Illustration 1, a.   Ready Position Illustration 1, b.

Then move your right leg out parallel to your body and have your feet about your own shoulder's width apart, at the same time close your fists and bring your hands to the front of you as in illustration 1, b.

Always Inhale through the nose at the start of the movement, exhale from the mouth at the end. This should be on every move throughout this book. At some stages it will be necessary to kiai (shout) at the end of a movement. I will advise on this as I proceed through the various techniques.

Now I am ready to begin

Fighting Stance

Fighting Stance Illustration 2, a   Fighting stance Illustration 2, b.

All stances are important but I class this as being the most important one as it is the one that your opponent will first see.

To get into a fighting stance from the ready position, I bring the left leg forward and raise my hands up to a guard position as in illustration 2,a and 2, b..

The feet should be about shoulder width apart, front foot turned inward. Reduce as much visible target area as possible so stand side on. I adjust my body weight so that I feel that am on the on the balls of my feet but I do not lift up on my heels. This will allow me to move fast.

The guard position is so important, one from the attackers point of view and second for your own protection. I have my hands up and arms crossed by the wrists as in illustration 2, c.

Illustration 2, c.
Correct arm position for guard up in fighting stance

With my left foot forward my front arm will protect my spleen. The back arm will protect my heart, liver and solar plexus. I have my fists closed but I do not clench them. I drop my chin down and relax the in the shoulders. Never have your hands open, your fingers would be vulnerable to attack. Also keep your hands just below your chin. If you bring your hands any higher I would see the as an opportunity to attack your hand first by punching your hands into your face.

Practice the fighting stance on both sides. Right and left. Every technique should be practiced on both sides. Now don't give the age old excuse you are right handed and that you find it awkward on the left. The attacker out in the street will not offer you any sympathy. So become ambidextrous like all good martial artists' have to be.

Rising Block And Forward Stance

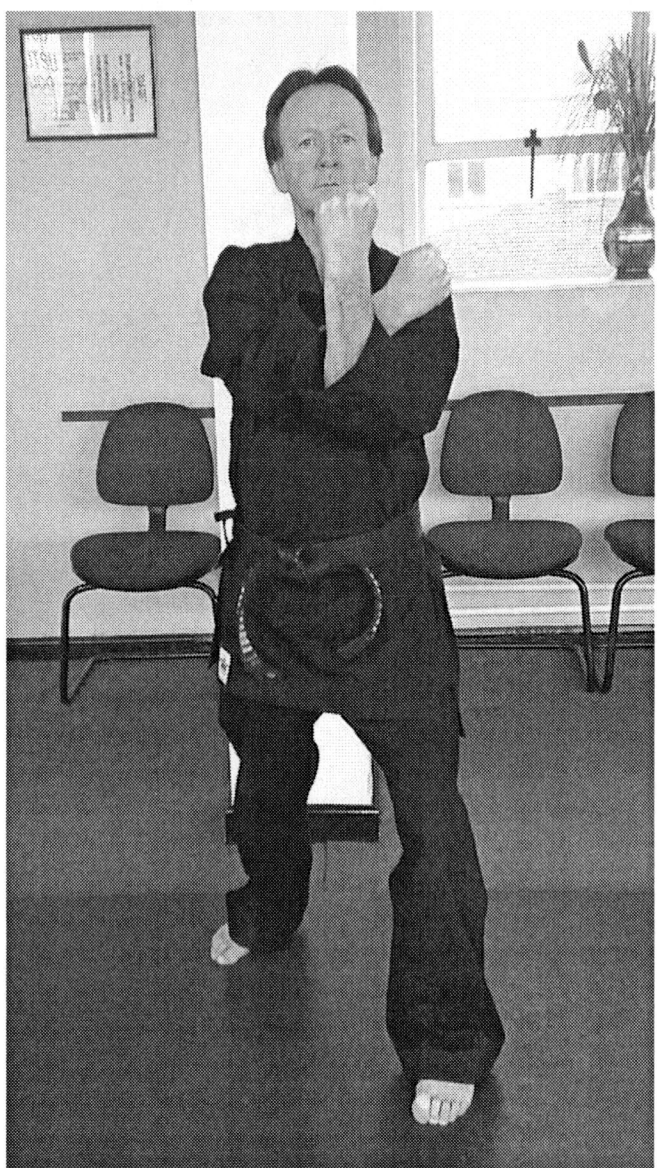

Illustration 3, a.

Stand in the ready position and advance the left leg forward at the same time raise the left arm and pull the right hand back to the hip. As you raise your left arm have that arm in front of your right, as in illustration 3, a. Take the left arm up straight and finally rolling it as you do the block. Your left arm should now be above your head with the hand higher than the elbow as shown in illustration 3, b.

The hand on the hip is called prepared position (that is prepared to strike) Always have your back foot flat. Do not come up onto your toes. The width of the stance will depend on your height. The taller you are the wider your stance, the shorter you are narrower your stance. As a general rule do not go low or to high just feel comfortable and that you are in a strong stance.

Rising block and forward stance. Illustration 3, b.

Testing your techniques. It is very important that you have confidence in your ability this is one way that will help. It also shows the strength and weaknesses of you techniques. On the down side your partner can demoralize you if he/she is much stronger then you are. Try to work with someone who can bring your ability on, it will pay vast dividends in the long run.

Testing the forward stance and rising block for strength. With a partner, one of you gets into the forward stance and completes the rising block. The other person then tests you by standing in front of you and placing both hands on your blocking arm and trying to pull down. You should be able to stop your partner easily if you have got this technique right.

The rising block will deal with an attack aimed from a blow being delivered to the centre of your head. This is only the basic position, when you have got the idea of this you will then learn the block strike. Block strikes are practiced with a partner and you can see these by looking at the actual attacks and defences section of this book.

Remember to practice left and right side.

Reverse Outside Forearm Block, Forward Stance

Illustration 4, a

Reverse outside forearm block and forward stance
Illustration 4, b.

Stand in the ready position raise your arms up left over right as in illustration 4, a. Move your left arm to your left side and pull your right back to your hip in the prepared position. As you are moving your arms step forward into the forward stance. As in illustration 4, b.

The Reverse outside forearm block deals with an attack to the side of your head from a blow where the attacker has had to make the distance between you by making a big step.

It is the outer edge of your arm that you use to block with.

Testing the reverse outside forearm block. With a partner, one of you takes the outside forearm block and forward stance position. The other person now stands in front of you and places both hands on your blocking arm and tries to pull towards you. If you are doing the technique correctly your partner should not be able to move you.

Inside Forearm Block, Forward Stance

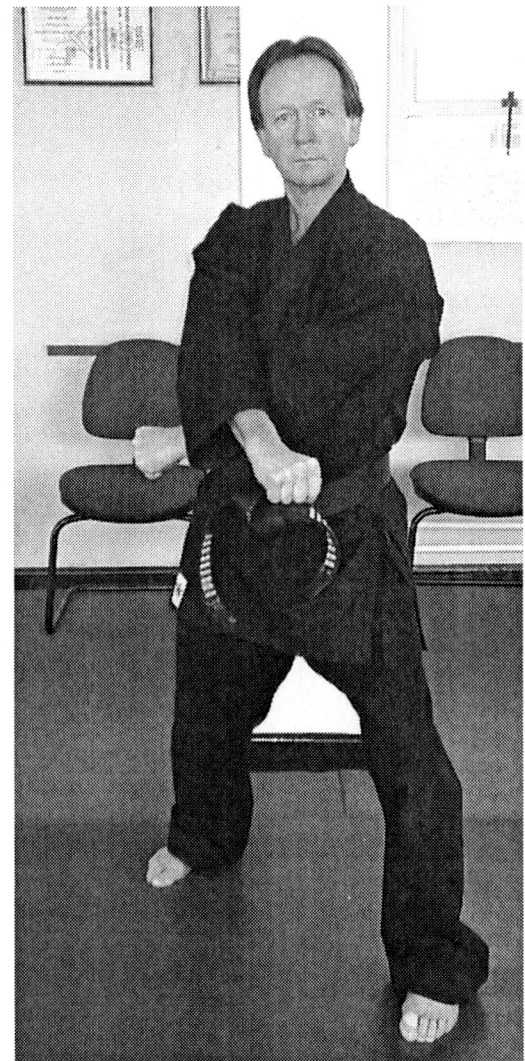
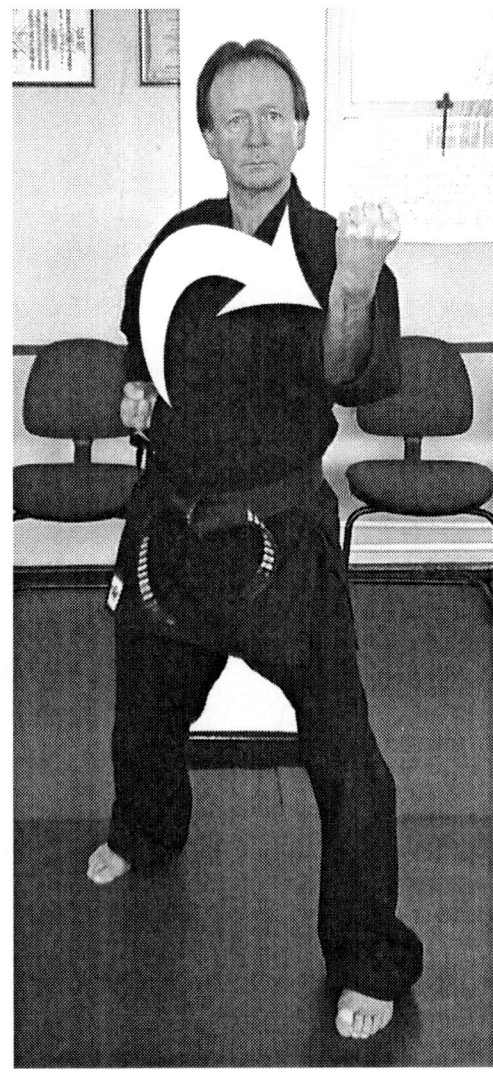

Illustration 5,a.

Inside forearm block and forward stance
Illustration 5, b.

The inside forearm block is done by first standing in ready position. Advance your leg to forward stance, as you are doing this cross your left arm in front of your right, as in illustration 5, a.

Now pull your right hand back to the prepared position and move your left arm to the inside forearm block position in illustration 5, b.

The inside forearm block is used in close quarter attacks where the attacker throws a punch to the side of your body or side of your head.

Testing the inside forearm block. With a partner one of you get into the inside forearm block position and forward stance. Your partner stands in front of you and places one hand on your left arm the other on your right hand and tries to move you. If you are the correct position your partner will not be able to move you.

Outside Forearm Block, Forward Stance

Illustration 6, a.

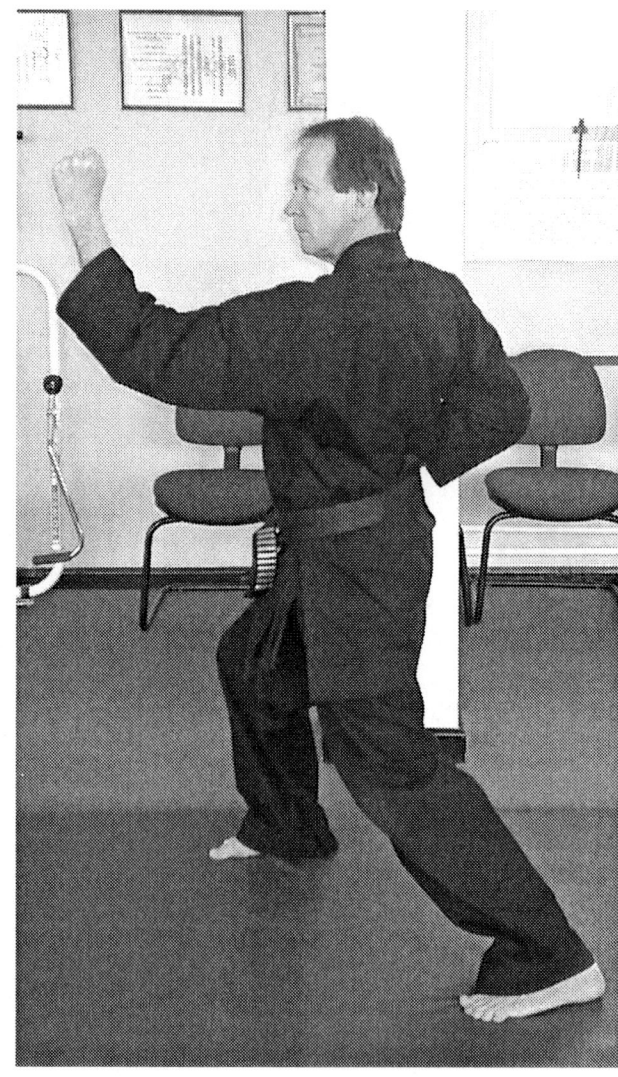

Illustration 6, b. Outside forearm block and forward stance

The outside forearm block is done by first standing in the ready position, raising your arms up to your left side as in illustration 6,a.

Advance your left leg to the forward stance position and the swing your arms to your right side, pulling your right hand back to the preparation position and your left arm into the inside forearm position. As you swing your arms across your body you also have to switch your weight from your front leg to your back leg. You end up with your back leg bent in a reverse stance. Take particular note of the change of stance from Illustration 6, a to illustration 6, b

Downward Sweeping Block, Straddle Stance

Illustration 7.

To do the downward sweeping block and straddle stance, stand in the ready position. Now step back with your right leg into a deep straddle stance. Have your feet parallel, toes gripping the Mat/floor. The outer edge of your feet should push into the mat/floor

As you step back pull your right hand to your hip in the prepared position and with your left hand drop it into the downward sweeping block position.,

How wide should your straddle stance be, well I recommend about two of your own shoulders width's is more than reasonable. The depth will vary according to the attack.

Just a reminder, practice both sides.

The downward sweeping block and straddle stance is an excellent defence against various kicks and also low strikes. The straddle stance is incorporated in many of the defence that I teach. Look at the defences from front and rear strangulation in this book to see how valuable the straddle stance is.

Testing the downward sweeping block and straddle stance. You and your partner needs get into a mirrored position in the downward sweeping block and straddle stance. That is to say that you are is a stance with your left leg forward your partner needs to have their right foot forward. Now both of you make forearm contact and push against each others forearm. You should both feel strong if you are doing this technique correct.

James Moclair

Lunge Punch, Forward Stance

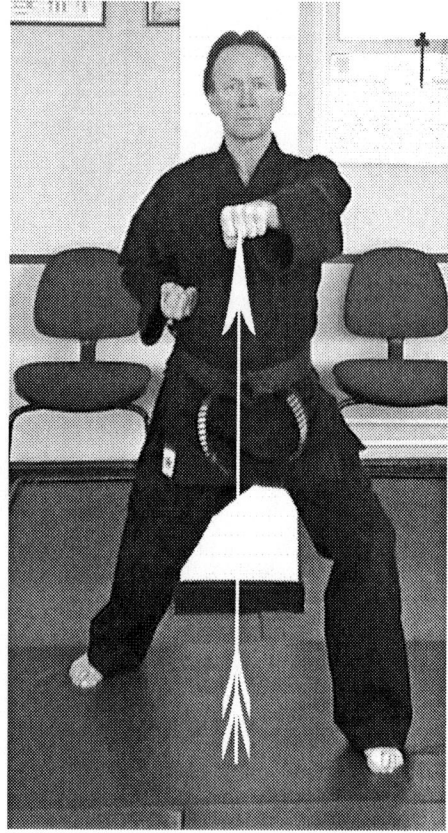

Illustration 8, a.   Lung punch. Illustration 8, b.

The white line on this illustration indicates the centre of the body and the correct position for the punching hand

The lunge punch is done by standing in the ready position. Pull both arms across you body at about waist height so you end up with your left arm sitting on your hip in the prepared position and your right arm across your stomach. Now step forward into forward stance while punching out with your left hand. Your right hand needs to be pulled back to your right hip in the prepared position as in illustration 8,a.

Make sure your punching hand is to the centre of the body and that your shoulders are square. This is important for power.

When you are punching your hand wrist and arm need to be in a straight line so that you do not damage your wrist or hand and always have a small bend in your elbow. Never lock your arm out straight. The small bend in your elbow has two benefits, one it stops damage to your elbow and two your arm is stronger with a small bend in the elbow. Look up the unbendable arm theory in an aikido book. Always have your thumb out and in the correct position. Refer to illustration 8,a, 8,b and 8,c.

Remember to practice both sides. I'm nagging you again.

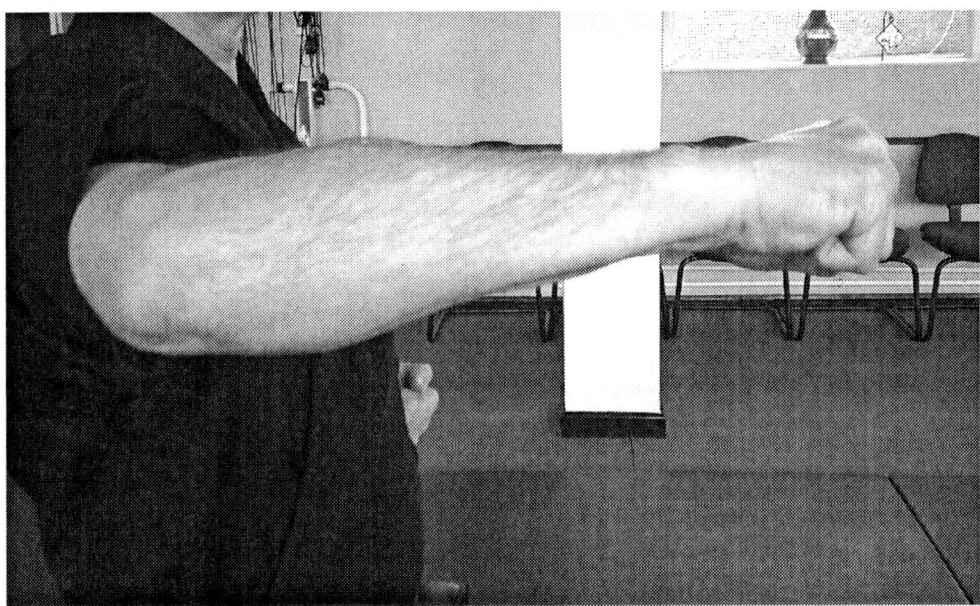

Lunge punch, correct hand position Illustration 8,c.

The area of your fist that you use to strike with is the first two knuckles, (Fore fist). As shown in illustration 8, d.

Striking area for fore fist. Illustration 8, d.

This is a basic position and other variations can be done once you master the basics.

Striking with the two knuckles gives you maximum impact. The idea behind this is the smaller the area you hit with maximises the impact. So if you hit with the whole of your fist it would not have the same impact as if you hit with two knuckles. Another way to look at this is if you had boxing gloves on the impact would not be so great as if your were a bare knuckle fighter.

Testing the lunge punch and forward stance. Again you will need a partner, come into the lunge punch and forward stance, have your partner stand in front of you and place one hand on the punching hand their other hand on your hand in the prepared position. Now get them to push. If your technique is right you should be as solid as a rock.

Now it is time for you to add a Kiai (shout) to the lunge punch. Stand in ready position. Inhale deeply through your nose, step forward into forward stance and pull your arms across your body and then Kiai (shout) as you do the lunge punch.

You do not shout out the word "Kiai" but make a natural sound. Every one has a slightly different sound. I use the word "shout" loosely to give a new reader with no martial arts experience an idea of what you do. The kiai is the essence that makes the art work. You must practice kiai as much as any other technique.

The Kiai will enhance the power of the lunge punch tremendously. It gets your mind and body to work as one, unites your spirit. It can also startle an attacker. How does this work? Simply you are at your strongest when you exhale. Now I have I test for you to try out this theory.

Again you will need a partner, come into the forward stance and lunge punch position. Have your partner stand in front of you and place both hands on your lunge punch hand. You now need to take a deep breath in through you nose.

As you exhale get your partner to push as hard as they can, you should immovable. Now try the same but this time "inhale" while your partner is pushing against your lunge punch arm. You will be pushed back immediately. Try the same test but this time kiai. You should be even stronger. Kiai can now added to all your techniques.

Practice the lunge punch on focus pad or similar striking pad or punch bag. To start with just do light strikes. Build up your punching power gradually. It is easy to skin your knuckles, so be careful when hitting the pad or bag. Hit it square on and do not skim your punching hand across the surface.

If you practice any techniques on a punch bag for safety always get someone to hold the bag while you practice on it.

Conditioning the hands for impact and developing calluses on the knuckles are shrouded by lots of myths within the karate world. Children should never attempt any type of conditioning their bones are still in the development stages. As an adult if you wish to toughen the striking area of your hands. You can start with bare knuckle light contact on a punch bag or striking pad. Build the power up slowly it will take time to condition the hands. You can also try knuckle press ups, on a hard surface. If you are not very strong do the press ups on your knees. Now that is as far as anyone need go for conditioning. In time it will get good results without deforming your hands or destroying the knuckle joints.

Reverse Punch, Forward Stance

Illustration 9, a.   Illustration 9,b.

To do the reverse punch start in the ready position, pull both hands across you body to the right side and step forward with your left foot in forward stance as in illustration 9,a.

Now pull your left hand back to the prepared position and punch out with your right hand. As in illustration 9, b.

Reverse punch forward stance. The white line on this illustration indicates the centre of the body and the correct punching position.

The punching hand should be to the centre of your body and your back foot should be flat with your toes on your back foot facing forward.

Testing the reverse punch and forward stance. With a partner, come into the reverse punch and forward stance, have your partner stand in front of you and place one hand on the punching hand their other hand on your hand in the prepared position. Now get them to push. If your technique is right you should be as solid as a rock.

Try the reverse punch with a Kiai (shout)

You can also practice the reverse on focus pad or similar striking pad or punch bag. To start with just do light strikes. Build up your punching power gradually. Make sure that you do not skin your knuckles.

I have to say his again, practice both sides.

Fighting Stance Into Front Jab

Fighting stance and front jab. Illustration 10

Bring your left leg forward and hands up into the guard position a practiced in illustration 2, a. From the fighting stance position advance your left forward and jab with your left hand. Keep your back hand up in the guard position as in illustration 10.

Once you have completed the jab return to fighting stance immediately.

When you do the jab do not lock your arm out straight, remember to always have a small bend in your arm for safety.

Try the jab with a Kiai (Shout)

You can also practice the jab on focus pad or similar striking pad or punch bag. To start with just do light strikes, Build up your punching power gradually. Make sure that you do not skin your knuckles.

Don't forget to practice right and left.

When you first start to do kicks get a partner and an appropriate pad for kicks. Never kick into thin air, you could hurt yourself badly this way. The pad offer's resistance and stops you over stretching. Over the years I have meet hundreds of ex martial artist's who have had to give up training due to knee injuries and torn muscles. They all tell the same story, "The instructor would get us to do our kicks into thin air" My advice to them is, sue the instructor for damages. My opinion of these so called Instructors is that they are not instructors they are "destructors"

Clothing and the type of shoes you wear will affect your kicking ability. If you wear trousers and they are tight you will not be able to lift your legs properly, tight skirts would have the same restrictions. I am not telling you to go out and buy a new wardrobe. I am just trying to put karate in the street into a real prospective.

High heel shoes would cause kicking problems as this would affect your centre of balance. Any jumping or spinning kick would indeed be very hazardous. Shoes with a smooth sole could cause you to slip in wet conditions. And shoes with a heavy tread on the sole. This may cause problems with traction and restrict the initial start of the kick.

Terrain and the weather will also change your kicking ability. Let me give you a worse case scenario. You are facing an attacker and you are uphill of this person. And to make it worse it is winter with patches of black ice and it is snowing. Wow now we are in a very challenging situation A Jumping spinning crescent kick would certainly end up with you on your backside.

Within my Kempo Karate system you are taught how to kick low, mid range and high range kicks are an option for those how have the extra flexibility. When I first started karate, the emphasise on kicks, was for power, high kicks have become popular with the introduction of sport. Rules in competitions do not allow very low kicks so every one has to kick high. Martial Art movies have also influenced the flashier kicks. I am highly amused at the martial artist who stands on one leg and flicks their kicks out repeatedly with no power in the kick They seem to think this is good and skilful ?. If I see one of my students flicking a kick out, I tell him/her "Don't be a flicka be a Kicka".

If you want to achieve more flexibility or possibly end up doing the splits then I recommend that you invest in a stretching machine. I do not recommend a cheap one, go for one that operates smoothly. If you join a good Dojo (Club) they will probably have a good range of stretching machines

To achieve more power in your kicks try the stretch bands on the market. They are excellent. They are made from surgical elastic and offer good forward and backward muscle resistance. You should be able to purchase them from any good martial arts outlet, shop or through mail order.

Start your kicks low and slow, let your legs warm up first. If you are new to martial arts keep your kicks low and slow until you are familiar with the techniques. I know it is tempting to blast your kicks out but you only have to get the kick wrong once and then you pay the price.

Front Kick

Stand in fighting stance, left leg forward. Raise your right leg up with your knee bent, at the same time curl up the toes on your right foot. Keep both hands up in a guard position as this not only protects you, it also helps greatly with your balance. Illustration 11, a shows the start of the front kick.

Starting the front kick, illustration 11, a

Now thrust forward and strike the pad with the ball of your foot. As shown in Illustration 11, b.

Front Kick Illustration 11, b.

Once you have done the front kick return to fighting stance immediately.
It is important to keep your hands up in a guard position while you do the kick for two reasons, one is to protect you from counter attacks and two is that keeping your guard up also helps with your balance.

On the subject of balance when you do the front kick bend a little on your supporting leg, this lowers your centre of balance. Always keep you supporting legs foot flat on the floor. If you lift your foot up on your supporting leg you will be of balance and it reduces the power of the kick.

When I watch someone doing a front kick, and they coming up onto their toes on the supporting leg. It is a good indication that they are over stretching themselves. I normally tell them not to kick so high and that normally sorts the problem out.

Breathing with your kicks is very important, at the start of the kick inhale through your nose as you execute the kick breath out sharply. As you get better at kicking start to add a kiai.

The front kick using the ball of you foot is a good all round kick for defence work.

I know you might think that I had forgotten to mention, practice on both sides.

A Breath Of Fresh Air

Side Kick

Stand in fighting stance, left leg forward. Raise your right leg up bending from the knee and drop your right arm down to help with counter balance and start to pivoting on your left foot as in illustration 12,a.

Starting the side kick Illustration 12, a.

Continue pivoting so that your foot rotates 180 degrees around and thrust your right leg out striking with the heel of your foot. As in illustration 12, b.

Side kick Illustration 12, b.

Return to fighting stance immediately upon completion of the side kick.

This kick takes a lot of practice, the rotation of your foot 180 degrees is very important for power and balance. Balance is further enhanced by dropping your arm down by your side as illustration 12,a.

Balance can be tweaked a notch more by having a small bend in your supporting foot.

From a street point of view I favour the heel of the foot as a good general all round strike in side kick. Their are however a couple of other options, you can use the edge of your foot or the ball of your foot. You would use the options for striking different targets on the body.

Using the edge of the foot in the side kick can be problematic. If your shoes have a big heels or thick soles may injure your ankle joint because that part of the shoe strikes first and puts enormous pressure on the ankle joint. So be careful.

Practice both sides and don't forget to breathe with your kicks.

Round House Kick

Stand in fighting stance, left leg forward. Raise your right leg up and have your both arms up to help maintain balance. As shown in illustration 13,a.

Starting the round house kick Illustration 13, a.

Pivot on the left foot until your foot has rotated 180 degrees and at the same time thrust your right leg in an upward arc so you strike the pad with top of your foot, lower part of your shin. As you thrust the right leg out, drop the right arm down by your right side to help counterbalance your body, as shown in illustration 13, b.

Return to fighting stance on completion of the round house kick.

Round house kick Illustration 13, b.

This again is a difficult kick to master. The rotation of your supporting foot is the key to a successful round house kick. It also helps to get every other part of this kick right but with a little practice you will be soon be achieving spectacular kicks. All right spectacular might be the wrong word, how about good kicks

Generally the very top of your foot, lower part of your shin is quite a devastating kick if landed properly. There are also a couple of nice options. You can kick with the ball of your foot and also the edge of your foot. To do the options you must adjust the angle of your position in relation to the pad or bag that you practice on.

When doing a round house kick be careful of your toes, it is quite common to knock your toes up if you get the kick wrong so start with light contact

Oh yeah, practice on both sided and don't forget to breath or kiai when you kick.

Back Kick

Stand in the ready position, your back to the pad, look over your right shoulder. Bend slightly on your left leg and raise your right leg bending from your knee as in illustration 14,a.

Starting the back kick Illustration 14, a.

James Moclair

Keep your hands up in the guard position for balance. Now thrust your leg back making contact with the heel of your foot. As in illustration 14,b.

Back kick Illustration 14, b.

Return back to the ready position on completion of the back kick

Always look to the side that you are about to kick, that is to say if you are going to kick with the right leg look over the right shoulder and if you are going to kick with the left leg look over the left shoulder. Never look one way and kick the opposite way, this is extremely bad for the lower back.

I now have to state the obvious. The back kick is used when the attacker is to the back of you. It is an extremely powerful kick. Start by doing this kick slow, it is easy to pull or strain yourself if you are not used of this kick.

If you have difficulty keeping your balance, then bend slightly on your supporting leg. Another way to help do this kick is take a partner. Both of you face each other. Place both hand on your partners shoulders raise your knee up as in illustration 14, a. and then push back to the kicking position do this a few times and then try the back kick on your own. And do it both sides.

An initial common fault is that the person doing the kick misses the pad or bag completely and nearly takes their partners head off, so be careful.

Kicking With The Top Of Your Foot

Stand in fighting stance left leg forward. Raise your leg bending from the knee toes pointing to the floor. Now snap the kick upward and strike with the top of your foot as in illustration 15

Front kick using the top of your foot. Illustration 15

Return to fighting stance immediately after completion of the kick

The front kick using the top of your foot is pacifically used to kick to an attackers groin area. You do not have to kick high with this kick. For example, if the attacker is two metres tall then the maximum height that you would kick is one metre, half of the body height. If they are shorter still, kick to one metre for the ouch effect.

Front Kick Using The Heel

Stand in fighting stance, left leg forward. Keep your guard up and raise the right knee up as high as you can. To help the heel strike the pad, bend your ankle joint so your right heel points to the floor. As shown in illustration 16, a.

Starting the front kick using your heel. Illustration 16, a.

Now thrust your leg forward and strike the pad or bag with your heel as in illustration 16, b.

Front kick with heel. Illustration 16, b.

Once you have completed the heel kick return immediately to fighting stance.

Use the heel of your foot to strike to the solar plexus, stomach and thigh muscles. As kicks come this is quite a devastating kick. It is not meant to be a high kick so do not try any area above the solar plexus.

If your shoes have a good heel, this is an extra bonus. For the ladies or gents who wear high heel shoes, you could spear the attacker with this kick.

Remember to breathe with the kick and have a go on the other side.

Axe Kick

Stand in the fighting stance position left leg forward. Raise your right leg as high as you can keeping your leg straight as in illustration 17,a.

Starting the axe kick Illustration 17, a

At the kicks highest elevation, strike down using your heel to hit the pad as in illustration 17, b.

Axe kick. Illustration 17, b.

Return to fighting stance immediately on completion of the axe kick

Always keep your guard up when doing this kick. The guard position helps with your balance as well as your protection.

When doing an axe kick be careful of striking your heel down on the floor it can be very painful. Even on mats your heel can bottom through the mat and hit the solid floor. You can see in the illustrations that I have taken extra precautious

You can do the axe kick in three different approaches.

1: From fighting stance lift your right leg straight up, at its highest elevation drop the leg straight down.

2: From fighting stance swing your right leg high to your left side and then bring it to the centre and drop it straight down.

3: From fighting stance swing your right leg high to your right side at it highest elevation bring the leg to the centre and drop it straight down.

The reason for the three different approaches is that your attacker will not always be at the right position to do just the one position. People move around in fights and techniques have to adapt to the situation.

Practice all variations of the axe kick right and left and breath with your kicks.

The odd kiai would be nice.

Front Angle Kick

Stand in fighting stance right leg forward. Raise your left leg up bending from your knee. Your knee should point out to your right as in illustration 18, a.

Starting the front angle kick. Illustration 18, a.

Now push down striking with the heel of your foot as in illustration 18, b.

Illustration 18, b.

Return to fighting stance as soon as you finish the front angle kick.

Front angle kicking is meant for close quarter striking. Keep your guard up for balance and protection and do not over stretch yourself when doing this kick.

The front angle kick is used in striking the legs, thighs and in particular the knee.

Yes, practice both sides; keep up the breathing and kiai.

Breaking Your Fall

In the next section of this book I will be showing you defences from various attacks. In order for you to try them you must first learn to break your fall and nothing else.

Do not try any of the defences unless you have a mat area to practice on.

The breakfall works by slapping the mat with one or both arms. The mat area is made of reconstituted foam or similar shock absorbent material. As you hit the mat with your arm the mat absorbs the energy of your fall. You cannot breakfall on a hard surface, you will only injure yourself as you become the shock absorbent material. A good example of this is when people commit suicide by jumping of tall building. The fall does not hurt them, but the floor gets them every time.

Side Breakfall

Lie on your back on the mat area, bend your knees up and lift your head up. As in illustration 19,a. Keep your tongue away from your teeth

Note the angle of the arm Illustration 19, a.

Now lift your left hand up and slap the mat with your hand and forearm, as in illustration 19, b.

Illustration 19, b.

As soon as you hit mat pull your arm up immediately so that your arm does not take any shock. Now repeat the breakfall right and left. As you are practicing the breakfall breathe out sharply each time your hand hits the mat. Your breakfall arm should be at 45 degrees in relation to your body position. Do not bring your arms out straight inline with your body as this makes the breakfall ineffective.

Back Breakfall

Step back with your right leg so that your bottom touches your heel. Cross your arms over and tilt your head forward. As shown in illustration 20, a.

Getting ready to back breakfall Illustration 20, a.

Keep your tongue always away from your teeth. Breathe in through your nose and then drop back slapping the mat with both hands. As you land lift both legs in the air. This will help you return to fighting stance. As in illustration 20, b.

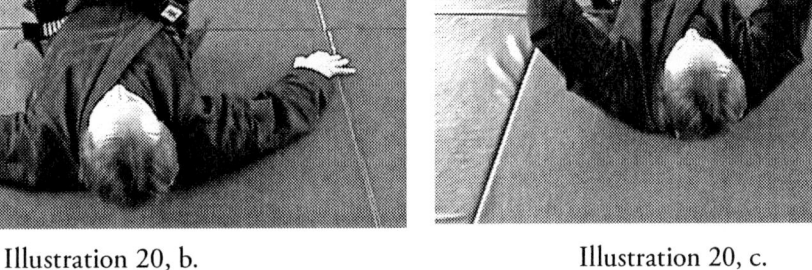

Illustration 20, b.   Illustration 20, c.

As soon as you hit the mat with both hands pull them back up quickly as in illustration 20, c. Once you have completed the back breakfall return to fighting stance.

"To Fight Or Not To Fight, That Is The Question"

In an attack situation you need to examine your options, here are a list of important street rules and advice that I consider vital to your survival.

1: You do not have to fight, you can run away. You are not a coward to do this, just simply surviving a bad situation. Remember that old saying. "He who runs away, lives to fight another day". Sometimes the odds are heavily stacked against you and to fight will result in you getting seriously hurt, you now have no option. Even great armies have through history had to retreat.

A question I am often asked is what I would personally do and my answer is always run away if possible. I also tell the person asking the question that I have done the potential attacker a big favour. I did not put him/her in hospital, I saved the national health department a fortune in health care and rehabilitation fees, I saved his/her family the grief of seeing their loved one on a life support machine. I saved the police and crown prosecution services a fortune in legal fees getting me prosecuted. I saved the prison services a fortune by me not being detained at Her Majesty's pleasure. And finally I save my family the humiliation of having a family member in Jail for G.B.H............. I think you might be getting the picture.

2: Try talking your way out. To do this takes skill and a little humility, humility is part of the essence of a martial art. Swearing, shouting and hurling abuse around is not the way forward. Try being calm, and be a little respectful. Even if in your opinion you are in the right. Try to look objectively at the other person's point of view and maybe offer a reasonable compromise. If this does not work then you can go to the next faze.

3: If the attack is a robbery or mugging it may pay you to just give the attacker what ever they are demanding. Your life is worth more than the contents of your purse or wallet. And I am sure all your family members would agree that you may have lost a little dignity but you are still alive and kicking.

One way to be safe is carry two purses or wallets with you. In one have a tiny amount of cash and a few expired credit cards and one or two other bits and peaces that are not of any value. In the other have your main supply of money and all the latest credit cards, drivers licence and so on. Carry the first one with hardly anything in it in the place where you would normally carry it and hid the other one away in a different place on your body. If you are mugged, hand over the first one with the small amount of cash in it. The mugger is happy until he looks at the contents and you get off lightly.

4: Strategy is an important factor in any fight. An excellent example of this is a famous samurai warrior was walking past a building site and several worker's started hurling abuse at him and wanted to fight him. The samurai knew their where too many to fight all at once, so he ran away. The workers gave chase and the samurai lead them to a small narrow foot bridge. This is where the samurai would take his stand. The bridge was only wide enough for one person at a time to enter it so when the workers tried to attack the samurai they could only do one at a time and not mob handed. They were then all quickly despatched.

If you visit a pub, club or restaurant or any such place where you feel that trouble might arise. Pay attention to the entrance and exits doors, they could be your bridge. Sitting in the centre of a room is a big mistake, you could be attacked in a 360 degree radius. Sit or stand with your back against a wall. If trouble does raise its ugly head you can use the fixtures and fittings of the establishment to assist you in your defence strategy.............. Now sit back, relax and enjoy yourself.

As you go about your daily activities you should be conscious of areas of potential danger. Unlit alleyways, poorly lit car parks and late night cash points are just few of the places to avoid. Everywhere is potential danger, if you sense danger then act immediately by avoiding that place like the plague. I always rely on my senses.

5: Defending yourself has implications that will affect your social life. The following example is for the older readers however the rule applies to everyone. If a ruckus kicks off, lets say in your local pub and you are involved and have to defend yourself then you must leave that place as quick as you can and don't go back ever. And I mean ever. The reason is that the person or persons who you fought with will be out for revenge. "Revenge is sweet"

After the fight the other party may even shake your hand, buy you a pint and tell you that you are on their Christmas card list for life. If you believe any of this then you are living on another planet. What will happen is you think it is all over, they do not. It will be festering in their brains and when you least expect it they will ambush you in some cowardly way and take their revenge.

6: It will be a miracle if you walk away from a fight unmarked. You must expect to take a few blows. You may think that taking up a martial art is going to make you invincible and that you will be so fast that you can dodge bullets. Well the truth is you are only human and like all human beings are lives are full of unpredictable events. What is even more unpredictable is a real fight.

Sometimes when you are training in martial arts you get a few bumps and bangs, this is all part of the mental toughening that will prepare you for the real thing.

7: I'm sure you have heard all those stupid saying like, "yeah he's going to be a push over." "This will only take a second." I'm going to put you in hospital pal" This is all banter and hot air and a mental way of trying to intimidate you. If you are intimidated by words alone then you have already lost the fight.

8: Remember that saying, "Sticks and stone will break my bones but names will never hurt me" Well I have to say that this saying is a load of rubbish. Just think how many fights have started by calling someone a name.? If someone calls you names do not be goaded into a fight. You cannot legally justify giving someone a good hiding for calling you a name. Maybe if you took the sticks and stones the saying literally there is a lot of wisdom in it.

9: You cannot do pre-emptive strikes; it will only get you in trouble with the boys in blue. I know that it's tempting to get the first blow in. But you will pay the price and spend time reflecting on your actions at her majesty's pleasure.

10: I have an exclusion zone that restricts me and my students from striking an attacker in the following areas, eyes, nose and mouth. I will deal with each of these areas so that you can understand the reasons why.

Firstly the eyes, it is morally wrong to deliberately injure the eyes or blind someone. You would be taking away one the most valuable assets that human being have, a persons sight. The eyes cannot be replaced. Legally you would probably end up in crown court trying to justify your actions to a judge and jury. And if they thought for one minute you were not fighting for your life and think you know what the outcome will be.

Striking someone on the nose normally has the effect that the nose will bleed quit profoundly. This will result in you also having their blood on you. In today's society we have to be more conscious of things like aids. What if the attacker that you just struck has A.I.D.S. I mentioned earlier that it would be a miracle if you walked any from a fight unmarked, you may also be bleeding. The interaction of blood could be fatal and not apparent immediately. Bear in mind that being attacked is not just what happens on you own door step. We all travel abroad a lot more than we use to. Some of the countries open for tourism have one out of six people with aids.

The mouth also falls into the A.I.D.S category but also has another potentially serious killer Hepatitis B. This is carried in the mouth in saliva. Punching someone in the mouth and maybe breaking your own skin could result in you getting one of the two diseases. You may win this fight but in five years time you could be fighting for your own life.

Also in my exclusion zone is the head. I never teach anyone to kick someone in the head when they are down on the floor and stamping on someone's head is definitely out. You could quit easily kill someone by doing these despicable things. I teach people to how to defend themselves and to have a moral conscious. I do not teach people to break the law of the land or the laws of religions. "Thou shall not kill"

10: I am now almost ready to unleash you on the world and start with the basic techniques you can use in attack situation but have just I have one more rule.

The distance rule: When being confronted by an opponent try to keep a reasonable distance between you and the attacker. It is not always possible but I recommend about two metres apart. That way your attacker has to lunge at you giving you a little more time to respond. The distant rule works even better if you are two miles are better and two hundred miles is better still. Illustration 21 shows you the distance rule.

The two metre distance rule. Illustration 21

When, an attacker goes to throw a punch, kick, or any other blow. I deal with this initially with a block strike. A block strike is very different then a block

With the block strike you block and strike smashing through the arm or leg that is delivering the blow at you. This will cause the attacker immediate pain to the attacker. The block striking method I use is extremely powerful, so much so that you could break the attacking limb. From start to finish the block strike is done in one sweeping action.

Block striking is quite unique in that it will quite often get the attacker into a of balance position. Look through some of the illustrations where the block strikes are used.

The principal of delivering a punch, blow, or kick in karate is that you do not strike the surface. You aim your blow or kick way past the surface and follow through until you have completed the technique. This makes the strikes, punches and kick of karate extremely powerful.

If you have to use any of the defences in a real attack, you do not have to do the whole routine as demonstrated in this book. If the attacker has had enough lets say with the first block strike then you should stop at that. You do not have to go over board with your line of defence.

Defence From A Downward Blow

The attacker has armed himself and is going to strike you on the centre of your head with the weapon. Stand in a fighting stance left leg forward and apply the distance rule. As shown in illustration 22, a.

Illustration 22, a

As the attacker raises his right arm with the weapon in it and steps forward with his right leg, advance forward on your left leg into forward stance and rising block using your left arm. The attacking arm gains more power as it on its downward swing.

It is important to stop the blow as soon as you can and do not let the attacker arm pass any further than the attacker's own shoulder. As in illustration 22

The correct position to stop the downward blow attack Illustration 22, b.

Now carry you block strike through in one sweeping action as in illustration 23.

Look how of balance the attacker is.

Completion of the block strike Illustration 23

Now do a reverse punch with your right hand striking with the first two knuckles (fore fist) to the chin as in illustration 24

Reverse punch to the attackers chin. Illustration 24

A Breath Of Fresh Air

Kiai On The Reverse Punch.

Now step back and deliver a kick with your right leg using the top of your foot to the groin as illustration 25

Kick to the groin using the top of your foot. Illustration 25

Return to a fighting stance immediately after finishing the kick. This is so important because their could be more that one attacker and you have to show them that you are alert and ready to continue if they want to attack you.

Breathing when doing the defences is of paramount importance for power. In illustration 23 on the completion of the block and strike, breathe out at the initial point of contact with the attackers arm. In illustration 23 breathe out or kiai as you do the punch. In illustration 25 breathe out or kiai as you do the kick.

When practicing the defences it is good to have a regular partner as this will bring your technical ability along but it is also good to work with lots of different people.

As people come in all shapes and sizes you must get used of handling them all. The weight and size differences will get easer the more you practise.

Always treat your partner with respect and never intentionally hurt them. If you are constantly over zealous with your contact you will not keep that partner for long.

Side Blow, To The Head

The attacker will try to throw a round house punch to the side of your face. Apply the distance rule and stand in fighting stance left leg forward. As shown in illustration 26.

Illustration 26. The attacker is about to throw a side blow.

As the attacker advances forward on his right leg and pulls his right hand back to start his attack, move forward quickly into forward stance and block strike using your left arm and doing the reverse outside forearm as in illustration 26, a. Kiai as you block.

Stop the attackers arm before the arm passes the shoulder

Stop the side blow by using the reverse outside forearm block strike.

Note how of balance the attacker is.

Illustration 26, a.

Move in close to the attacker placing your right hand on the attacker left shoulder use your forearm to strike him under the chin as in illustration 26, b. Be careful when practicing the forearm strike it is a powerful strike. Make sure your practice partner keeps this tongue away from his/her teeth.

Striking the attacker, under the chin, use the forearm. Illustration 26, b.

Close up shot of strike under the chin using forearm. Illustration 26, b,a.

Now step past the attacker with the right leg driving him to the floor as in illustration 26, c. Kiai as you throw the attacker to the floor. Position yourself so that you are in a good target area to finish this routine.

James Moclair

Driving the attacker, to the floor Illustration 26, c.

Finish the move of by delivering a kick using the heel of your right foot to the groin area of the attacker's body. Kiai when doing the heel kick. As shown in illustration 26, d.

Delivering a heel kick Illustration 26, d.

When you throw a person to the floor they will land in various positions, so you will have to adjust your final strike to match the attacker's landing position.

A Breath Of Fresh Air

Quarter Stepping

Before I go to the next technique, I would like to explain about quarter stepping. This is a movement that is used to evade an attack. The attack could be a straight punch to your face or a knife attack where the attacker lunges straight at you.

To practice quarter stepping stand in fighting stance left leg forward as in illustration 27, a.

Quarter step start Illustration 27,a.   Quarter step middle. Illustration 27, b.

Advance your left leg forward and out at about a 20 degree angle as in illustration 27, b.

James Moclair

Now slide your right foot so that it is about you own shoulders width apart and pivot your body about 20 degree as in illustration 27, c.

Completion of the quarter step. Illustration 27, c.

It is very important that you practice the quarter step until you have a nice smooth movement. Once you have got the hang of this try practicing with a partner. Get your partner to slowly try to punch you in the face and us the quarter step to evade the punch. Timing is the key when evading the punch, with practise your timing will improve greatly. Once you have got the quarter looking good on the one side change over and practice on the other side.

A Breath Of Fresh Air

Straight Punch To The Face

The attacker will try to hit you, with a straight punch, to the face. Apply the distance rule and come into fighting stance left leg forward as shown in illustration 27.

Illustration 27.

James Moclair

As the attacker steps forward with the right leg and throws the straight punch with his right hand, quarter step to his outside and raise your left hand ready to use the outside forearm block strike as in illustration 27, a.

Quarter step to the outside of the attacker right arm. Illustration 28, a.

To show the outside forearm block strike more clearly I have changed my position around.

Use the block strike to attack the attackers arm just above the elbow joint, this should drive the arm away from you as shown in illustration 28, b.

Illustration 28, b.

Pull your block strike arm back to your left hip and do a reverse punch as in illustration 28, c. Kiai, when doing the reverse punch.

Illustration 28, c.

Finally, raise the right leg up and deliver a front angled kick to the rear attacker's knee as in illustration 28, d. Kiai as you strike with the front angle kick.

Delivering a front angled kick to the back of the attacker's knee. Illustration 28, d.

Once you have completed the angle kick return to fighting stance immediately.

Front Strangulation

As I have mentioned before it is not always possible to apply the distance rule. In the next attack, the attacker is trying to apply a front strangulation. The first thing to do is not panic, if you panic you will die. The neck muscles are quite strong, they holds your head in place. Practice tensing up your neck muscles, so that you can offer some resistance. However if you try the next technique you will see how easy it is to break out of the strangle hold.

The attacker places both hands around your throat, bring your left leg forward and come into a forward stance as in illustration 29, a.

Illustration 29, a

To start this defence, step back sharply with your left leg as far as you can and come into straddle stance and the same time strike hard the attackers left arm with your right arm as in illustration 29, b. Kiai as you strike the attackers arm. The stepping back as far as you can into straddle stance will break the attempted strangulation. As you will see in illustration 29, b, I have raised my left arm up this is for head protection. Sometimes as you step back sharply it pulls the attacker head towards you. The raised left hand is there to stop an accidental head collision.

Breaking the strangle hold. Illustration 29, b.

Continue to drive your right hand down so that it completely breaks the attacker's strangle hold at the same time extenuate your straddle stance as shown in Illustration 29, c. Both illustration 29, b and 29, c should be preformed in one smooth powerful movement.

Illustration 29, c.

Having a good stance and good posture is vital in giving power to punches, strikes and kicks. Stances are also a key item in helping you to do defend yourself. In many of the defence routines in this book you will see that a particular stance is employed to enhance the routine and stop the attacker from trying to achieve his goal. In most cases without the proper use of the stance the routine will only half work and out on the street this is a disaster.

Now deliver a hammer fist blow to the attacker's forehead and kiai. As shown in illustration 29, d

Hammer fist to forehead. Illustration 29, d.

To do a hammer fist strike close your fist tightly and use the flesh and muscle area on the side of your hand bellow the little finger. Make sure you do not strike and hit with the little finger and always have a small bend in your elbow when you make contact. The bend in the elbow takes pressure of the elbow joint. You can achieve a tremendously powerful strike with the hammer fist.

Try practicing the hammer fist right and left hand on a striking pad

Finally using the heel of your foot, do a stamping kick to the attackers foot as in illustration 29, d. Kiai when you do the stamping kick.

Stamping Kick to attacker foot. Illustration 29, d.

Return to fighting stance as soon as you have completed the stamping kick.

When you are familiar with this defence routine on the one side, practice the same routine on the other side.

Rear Strangulation

Attacks can come at every conceivable angle, for the next attack the attacker will try to do a strangle from the rear. Remember do not panic, although the attacker has put his hands around the neck. The rest of your body is free and this is where you can use to apply the following techniques.

The attacker is trying to strangle from the rear, step back immediately with the left leg so you have a good posture as shown in illustration 30, a.

Rear Strangle Illustration 30, a.

Reinforced Elbow Strike

Step back with the right leg into a straddle stance, as you are stepping back strike hard with your right elbow into the attacker's solar plexus. Kiai as you strike with the elbow. I have reinforced the elbow strike. To do this close your fist on your right hand and place your left on it with the palm heel as in illustration 30, b.

Reinforced elbow strike. Illustration 30, b

The reinforced elbow strike will have loosened the attacker up nicely so you can easily passes your right arm under the attackers left arm and hook your right around his shoulder and draw his head forward. Illustration 30, c show the attacker been drawn forward using the right arm.

Illustration 30, c.

James Moclair

Keep the right arm wrapped around the attacker's left arm as close to the shoulder as you can get it. This is not a lock, just a control procedure. Use your left forearm to strike the attacker in the nape of the neck, as shown in illustration 30, d.

Illustration 30, d. Stamp kick to attacker's foot. Illustration 30, e.

Finally, using your heel do a stamping kick using the heel of your foot to the attackers foot and kiai. This will immobilise him and will give you a chance to get away. As in illustration 30, e.

When you are familiar with this defence routine on the one side, practice the same routine on the other side.

Stamping kicks are my favourite kicks, they are easy to do and very effective. You can do them in confined places where other kicks would be impossible to perform. Hey here's a happy thought for you, a stamping kick is one of the few kicks that you can do while sitting on a toilet without embarrassing yourself. Mind you it would slightly embarrassing to be attacked while sitting on the loo, ………but it could happen.

Front Bear Hug, Arms Pinned

The attacker is going to try to pin your arms in a bear hug, step back with your right leg as far as you can into a forward stance and place your hand on the attacker hips, this will stop him getting a tight grip on you. Also drop your head to the side to avoid an accidental head collision as in illustration 31, a.

Attacker trying a bear hug Illustration 31, a.

Bring your right knee up and sharply knee the attacker in the solar plexus and kiai. (The stomach or groin area a also valid target areas) Illustration 31, b shows the knee kick..

Knee kicking the attacker. Illustration 31, b.

Without putting your knee kicking foot onto the floor step back with your right foot and draw the attacker forward with the left arm under the attackers right arm as in illustration 31, c.

Drawing the attacker forward. Illustration 31, c.

Finally deliver an elbow strike to the centre of the shoulder blades as demonstrated in illustration 31, d. Kiai when you strike with the elbow.

Elbow strike to the centre of the shoulder blades. Illustration 31, d.

Return to fighting stance immediately upon completion of the elbow strike.

Don't forget to practice this routine on the opposite side.

Front Bear Hug, Arms Free

In the next attack, the attacker has come from the front, left leg forward and will try to do a bear hug with the arms around the waist. Step back as far as you with your right leg into a forward stance as the attacker approaches you. Keep your head to one side to one to avoid an accidental head butt. Take a hold of the attackers arms with both hands as in illustration 32, a.

Step back as the attacker tries to do a bear hug. Illustration 32, a.

Move your right foot forward and throw the left leg back as far as you can, pulling on the left arm and pushing with the right. The attacker is now being pulled of balance as shown in illustration 32, b and also in illustration 32, b,a.

Getting the attacker off balance. Illustration 32, b

Illustration 32, b, a.

James Moclair

Keep pulling with the left arm and pushing with right and throw the attacker to the floor. Keep your left arm wrapped around the attacker right arm and apply a lock to the back of the attackers elbow joint by levering upward. The right hand is transferred to the attacker's throat using the fingers to apply a pressure point into the carotid artery. As shown in illustration 32, c and in a close up in 32, c, a.

Illustration 32, c.

Illustration 32,c,a.

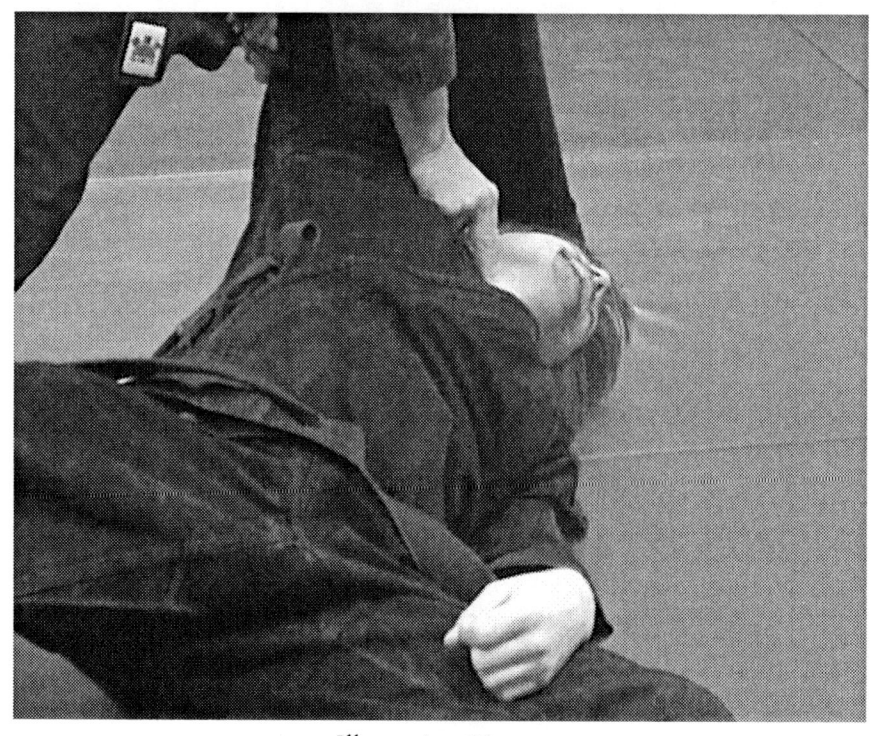

A Breath Of Fresh Air

The carotid artery is located in the neck along the side of the wind pipe. It is where you feel for a pulse. As shown in illustration 32, d. All pulse points on the body are also pressure points.

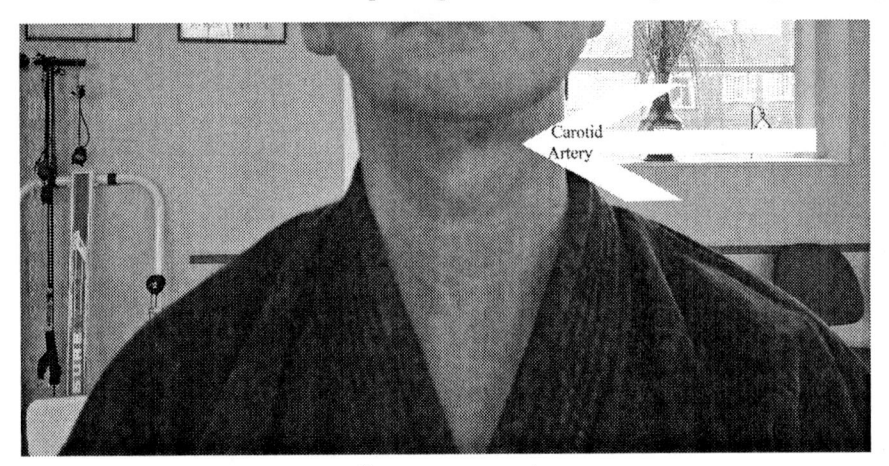

Illustration 32, d.

Keep the elbow lock on and punch with the right hand into the attacker ribs as in illustration 32, d. Kiai when you do the reverse punch.

Illustration 32, d.

Return to fighting stance as soon you have completed the routine.

Always expect an attacker to try to get out of a lock or control procedure. It is quite normal for them to try to resist any technique that you are applying. You have to keep control of them by applying more pressure to the lock and verbally warn them that if they resist they will get more pain. Now we have a problem, which is simple to resolve, what if they don't speak your language.

Well we all understand pain, pain is the universal language. So talk to the attacker in universal language.

There is however a limit to how much pain we will be willing to endure. If the pain from the lock you are applying becomes too great the attacker out of complete desperation will break their own arm or limbs trying to escape. It takes practice to get the right balance……and to start with a bit of luck.

Another thing to consider is that we all have different pain thresholds, alcohol and drugs really do affect the nervous system. What will be terrible pain for one person is hardly anything to another. You really have to treat everyone as an individual and hope that the attacker is not double jointed throughout their body…… Oh boy would that be a bomber.

Rear Bear Hug, Arms Pinned

In the next attack, the attacker has come from the rear and will try to restrain the arms with a rear bear hug. As soon as the attacker try's to apply the rear bear hug, bring both arms forward to a 20 degree angle. At the same time tense up the upper part of your body. This will restrict the attacker getting a tight hold on you. At the same time as you raise the both arms up move the right foot back so that you have good posture. As shown in illustration 33,a.

Rear bear hug Illustration 33, a.

Stamp kick with the right foot to the attacker's right foot. Kiai as you stamp kick. As shown in illustration 33, b.

Stamp kick to attacker foot. Illustration 33, b.

Now step back as far as you can with the right foot and reach down with both hands and take hold of the attacker's right leg at the ankle as shown in illustration 33, c.

Reach down and grab the attackers leg. Illustration 33, c.

Pull the attackers right leg upward sharply so that he becomes off balance and is thrown to the floor as in illustration 33, d.

Throw to the floor. Illustration 33, d.

Turn to face the attacker and with the right leg do a heel kick to the attacker solar plexus. As shown in illustration 33, e.

Heel kick to the attacker's solar plexus. Illustration 33, e.

Throw the attacker's right foot in the direction of his/her left shoulder, turning him/her onto his side as shown in illustration 33, f

Throwing the attacker's right foot helps to turn him onto his side. Illustration 33, f.

Now complete the routine by delivering a heel kick to the attacker's kidneys area as shown in illustration 33, g. Kiai when you do the heel kick.

Heel kick, to the kidney area. Illustration 33, g.

Return to fighting stance immediately after completion of the heel kick

Front Hair Pull

The attacker's next attack is a front hair pull as he approaches he grabbed a handful of hair from the front with his right hand. Come into a good posture immediately with the left leg forward. Bring the right hand up and clamp onto the attacker right hand making your forearm and the attackers forearm make contact. At the same time take the left hand and grip the attackers arm at the back of the tricep muscle.   As shown in illustration 34, a.

Griping the attackers arm, in a front hair pull attack. Illustration 34, a.

The close up illustration in 34, a, 1. This picture shows the correct hand positions for the right and left hand. It is important that you practice these hand grips, as you don't want be losing the front of your hair prematurely.

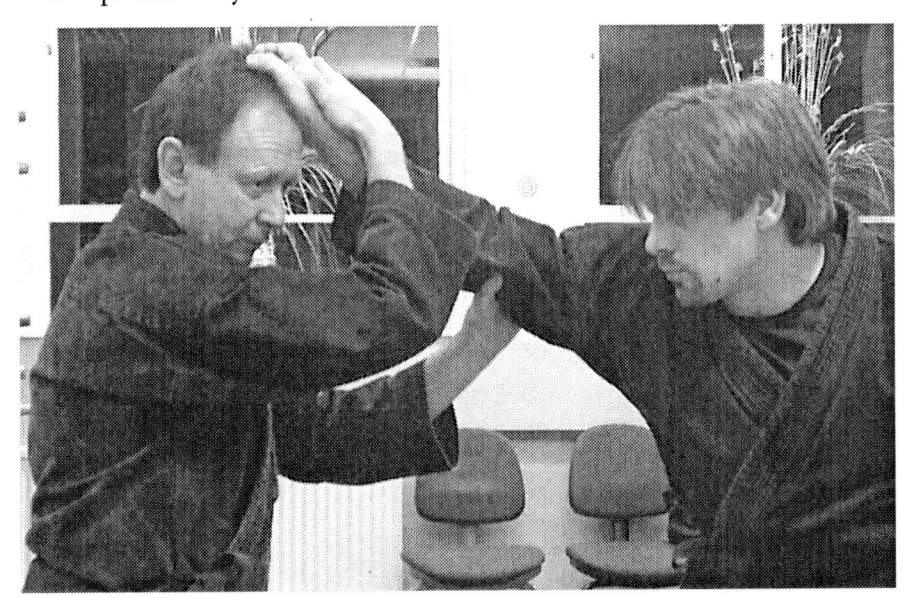

Illustration 34, a, 1.

Now, do a shin kick, to the attacker inside thigh muscle as shown in illustration 34, b. Kiai with the shin kick.

Shin kick to the inner thigh. Illustration 34, b.

Now the attacker is nicely loosened up. Bend the attacker wrist with you right hand and push with your left hand. This will result in a wrist lock being applied to the attacker wrist and he will be forced to release the hair as shown in illustration 34, c.

Applying a wrist lock to the attacker. Illustration 34, c.

A Breath Of Fresh Air

To help you get the wrist lock right study illustration 34, c,a. Note how my right hand is positioned on the attacker's right hand and that my left hand is just above the attacker's elbow joint.

The attacker's wrist and elbow are both bent at the respective joints and I am applying pressure by squeezing inwards with both my hands.

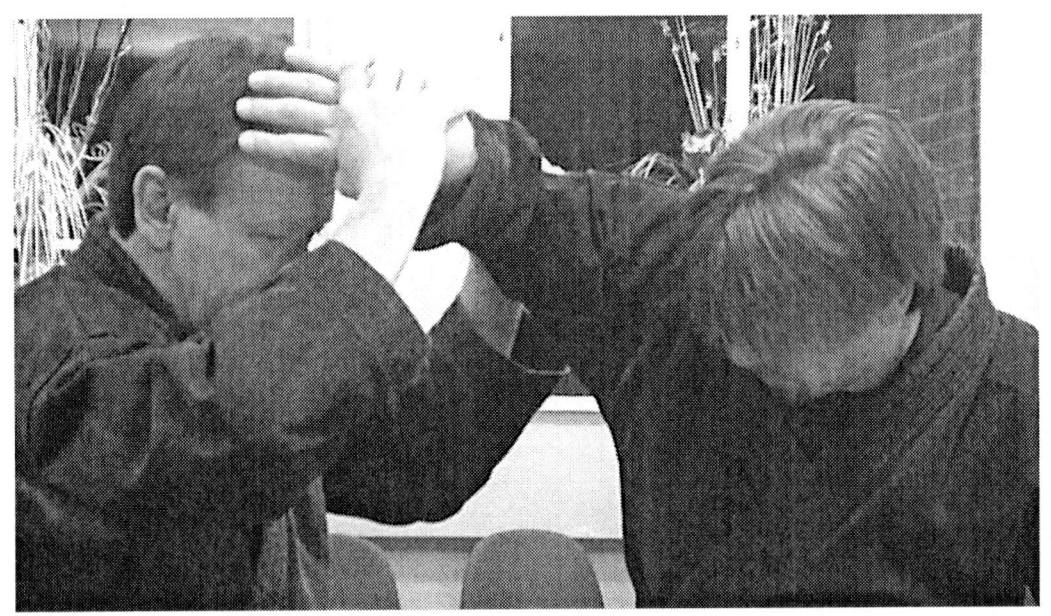

Illustration 34, c, a.

Bring your arms to about waist height this will draw the attacker forward. Keep the wrist lock on with the right hand and also put an elbow lock on the attacker arm with the left hand. As shown in illustration 34, d.

Applying a wrist and elbow lock.   Illustration 34, d.

Finally release the attacker arm and do a reverse punch to the attackers rib area as shown in illustration 34, e. Kiai with the reverse punch.

Reverse punch to attacker's ribs. Illustration 34, e.

I mentioned earlier in this book about the principal of karate's powerful strikes. You have to focus beyond the point of impact and blast through that area with the punch or strike. The same applies in the reverse punch as in illustration 34, e. The ribs are the initial contact area and you only stop the punch when you have completed the reverse punch technique.

Hair Pull, From The Rear

The attacker has grabbed a handful of hair from the rear with his right hand. Get into a good posture immediately. I have done this by stepping back with my right foot as in illustration 35, a.

Hair pull, from the rear. Illustration 35, a.

Bring your right hand up and clamp onto the attackers right hand. Have your elbow pointing forward as shown in illustration 35, b.

Clamping the attacker's hand, with right hand. Illustration 35, b.

Step back with the left leg into straddle stance and using the left arm elbow strike the attacker solar plexus as shown in illustration 35, c. Kiai with the elbow strike.

Elbow strike the attacker in the solar plexus. Illustration 35, c.

Now with the left hand take hold of the attacker right arm below the elbow joint. Bend the attacker's wrist with your right hand at the same time push with your left hand.

This will apply a powerful wrist lock and the method of applying it is identical to the front hair pull wrist lock. As shown in illustration 35. c. Also refer to illustration 34, c, a. for further help

Applying a wrist lock. Illustration 35, c.

Drop both your hands to waist height sharply to break the attacker balance keeping the lock on the wrist as shown in illustration 35, d.

Drawing the attacker off balance and keeping the wrist lock on. Illustration 35, d.

Finally release the attackers hand and do a reverse punch to his rib area as shown in illustration 35, e. Kai with the reverse punch

Finish with a reverse punch. Illustration 35, e.

Return to a fighting stance on completion of the reverse punch.

What I have covered so far in this book with the blocks, punches, kicks and defence routines is what is the grade requirement, within my kempo karate syllabus: for a novice to a white belt. I know it is a lot to take for a novice to get their fist belt, but I believe in laying a good positive foundation. Now I have something to build on, I can proceed to the next grade with slightly more advanced techniques.

Yellow Belt Syllabus

For additional mat safety I will start by explaining the techniques of rolling backward and forward. These should only be practice on a mat area and not on a hard surface.

Backward roll

Step back with the right leg and lower your bottom so that it touches the right heel. At the same time bring both arms out about 45 degrees and let the fingers of both hands touch the mats as shown in illustration Backward roll 1

Backward roll 1

Put the head to the right side, lie down on your back and bring the feet over the left shoulder. Use the arms as stabilisers as shown in illustration backward roll 2.

Backward roll 2

Land, kneeling on the left knee, toes curled upward. Have the right foot on the floor, and the hands coming up into guard position. As shown in illustration backward roll 3.

Backward roll 3

To finish the backward roll stand up in fighting stance right leg forward. As shown in illustration backward roll 4.

Backward roll 4

Forward roll

Step forward with the left leg and place the finger tips of the left hand by your big toe. The right hand is placed on the mats at about shoulder width apart as shown in illustration forward roll 1

Illustration Forward roll 1

Lift the right leg up and tuck it to your backside and lower the head down but do not touch the mat with your head. In this position you will now be able to roll forward. As shown in illustration forward roll 2

Illustration forward roll 2

As you come out of the roll you should land in a kneeling position with the right leg forward and the left forming what I call a tee shaped position as shown in illustration 3. The white arrow's on illustration 3 show what I mean by the tee position.

Illustration forward roll 3

To finish the forward roll, stand up in fighting stance right leg forward. Forward rolls can be practiced both sides so now get working on the left side.

Rising Cross Block And Forward Stance

Start by standing in the ready position, step forward with the left leg into forward stance and at the same time pull both hand back to your hips as shown in illustration 36, a.

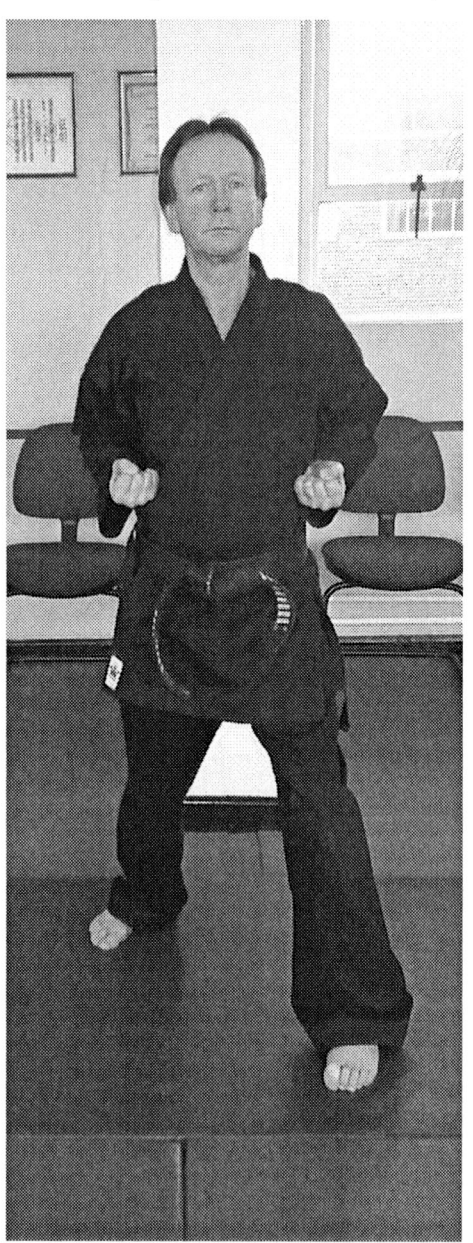

Starting the rising cross block.
Illustration 36, a.

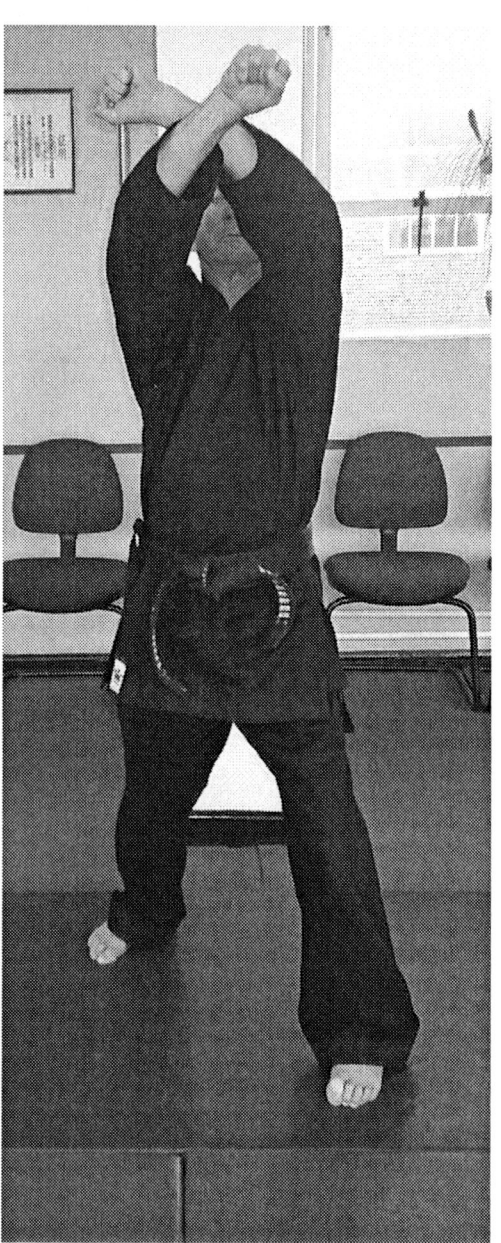

Completion of the rising cross block.
Illustration 36, b.

Raise both arms up sharply with the left on top of the right to complete the rising cross block as shown in illustration 36, b. and 36, d. Have your arms forearm to forearm and not wrist to wrist.

Rising cross block from the side Illustration 36, d.

Practice the rising cross block and forward stance right and left.

Testing the rising cross block and forward stance is done by taking a partner. You come into the rising cross block and forward stance position, left leg forward and left arm on top. Your partner stands in front of you placing their right arm in between the cross you have made with your arms. Get them to push down hard, your arms should solid and your stance immovable. Now try this on the other side.

I use the rising cross block and forward stance for close quarter blocking from a downward blow. It also leads nicely into arm locks as you will see when I show the close quarter defences later in the book.

When practising the rising cross block add a kiai Just as the arms cross for more power.

James Moclair

Downward Cross Block And Forward Stance

Stand in ready position and advance the left leg forward and the same time pull both of your hands back to your hips. As shown in illustration 37, a.

Illustration 37, a.

Now thrust both arms down sharply with the left hand on top of the right to complete the technique as shown in illustration 37, b.

Completion of the downward cross block and forward stance. Illustration 37,b

The downward cross block can be used for blocking both low kicks and low punches to the stomach.

When practising the downward cross block add a kiai just as the arms cross for more power.

Testing the downward cross block and forward stance is done by taking a partner. You come into the downward cross block and forward stance position, left leg forward and left arm on top. Your partner stands in front of you placing their right arm in between the cross you have made with your arms. Get them to push up hard, your arms should solid and your stance immovable. Now try this test on the other side.

Don't forget to practice the technique right and left.

Knife Edge Block Strike And Back Stance

Stand in the ready position, bring the left leg forward and pivot 45 degree's on your right foot at the same lift both your arms aiming them over your right shoulder as shown in illustration 38, a.

Starting, the knife edge block strike and back stance. Illustration 38, a.

Knife edge block strike and back stance. Illustration 38, c.

Bring both hands forward, having the right hand to the centre of your chest and the left striking out into the knife edge hand position. The hands should line up at the same angle. Seventy five percent of your weight should be in the left leg and twenty five percent in the right leg. Bend on the right leg so the knee is in line with the toes. The toes on the front foot should point directly forward as shown in illustration 38, c.

Try practising the technique with kiai's for more power.

Keep the thumbs at the side of the first finger and have each of your fingers slightly apart to avoid injury. Having each of the fingers apart avoids shock waves going through them when you make contact. The knife edge area is located below the little finger and is the fleshy and muscle part of the side of your hand as shown in illustration 38, d. Do not use the bone directly below the little finger. It can be easily broken.

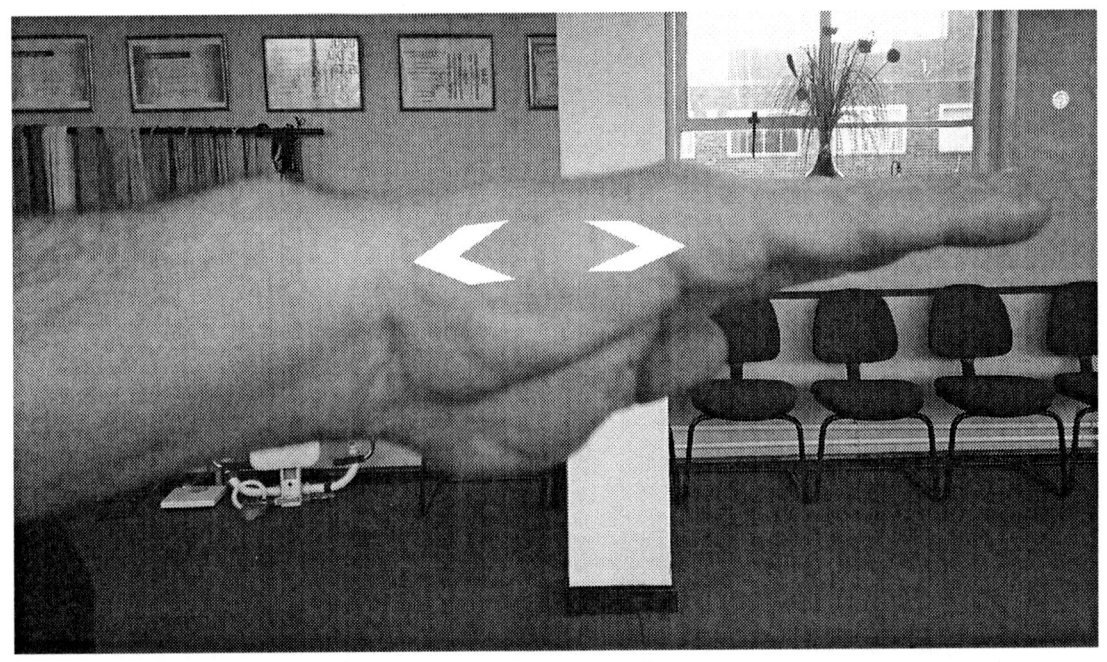

Between the arrows is the striking area for the knife edge hand strike

Illustration 38, d.

The knife edge block is an extremely powerful block strike that can be used to devastate muscles and also break bones. It is very versatile in its usage.

Testing the knife edge block and back stance. Take a partner and face each other in the knife edge block and back stance position. One of you should have the left leg forward the other the right toes pointing forward towards each other. Place the left hand against your partners right hand making contact with the knife edge part of the hand. Now both of you inhale through the nose, start to exhale slowly through the mouth and start to push against each other hands. If you are both doing the technique correctly, you should feel strong in the stance and knife edge block.

Cat Stance And Back Fist Strike

Stand in the ready position; turn the right foot 45 degrees to your right. Bring the left foot to the centre of the right foot balancing on the ball of the foot. The distance between the left and right foot will vary slightly due to different foot sizes but as a rule if you put the foot that you are balancing on flat on the floor the heel should just touch the other foot. At the same time that you move your feet bring the right arm out and the left arm hand goes close to the chest as shown in illustration 39, a.

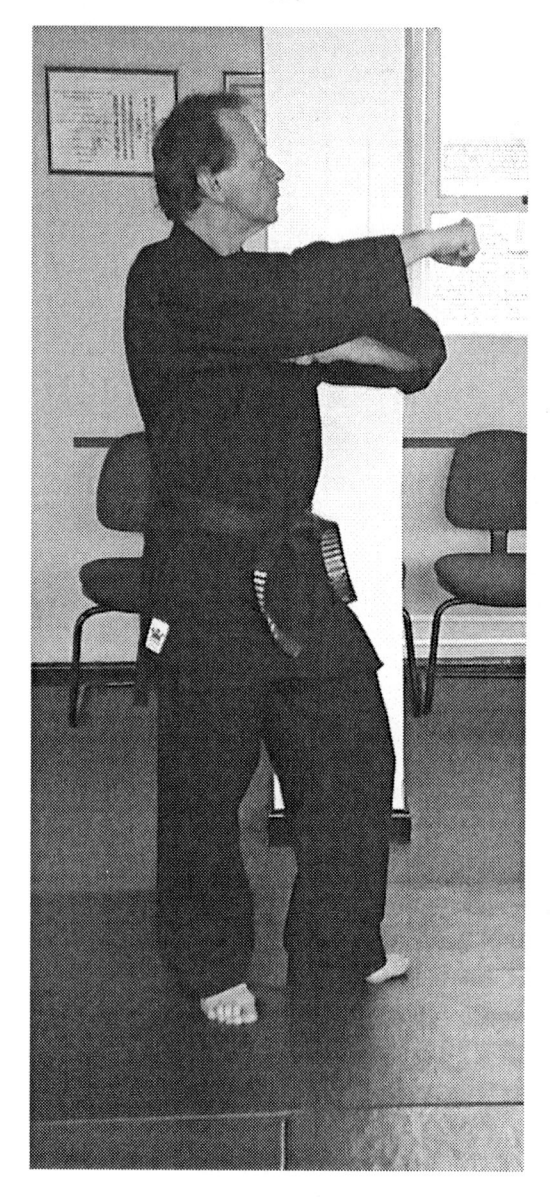

Starting the cat stance; and back fist strike.
Illustration 39, a.

Completion of the cat stance and back fist strike.
Illustration 39, b.

Now strike out with the left and pull the right hand to the centre of the chest as shown in illustration 39, b. Note the bend in the wrist for getting the hand into the write position for the strike.

The back fist strike is done by striking with the first two knuckles. As shown in illustration 39, b.

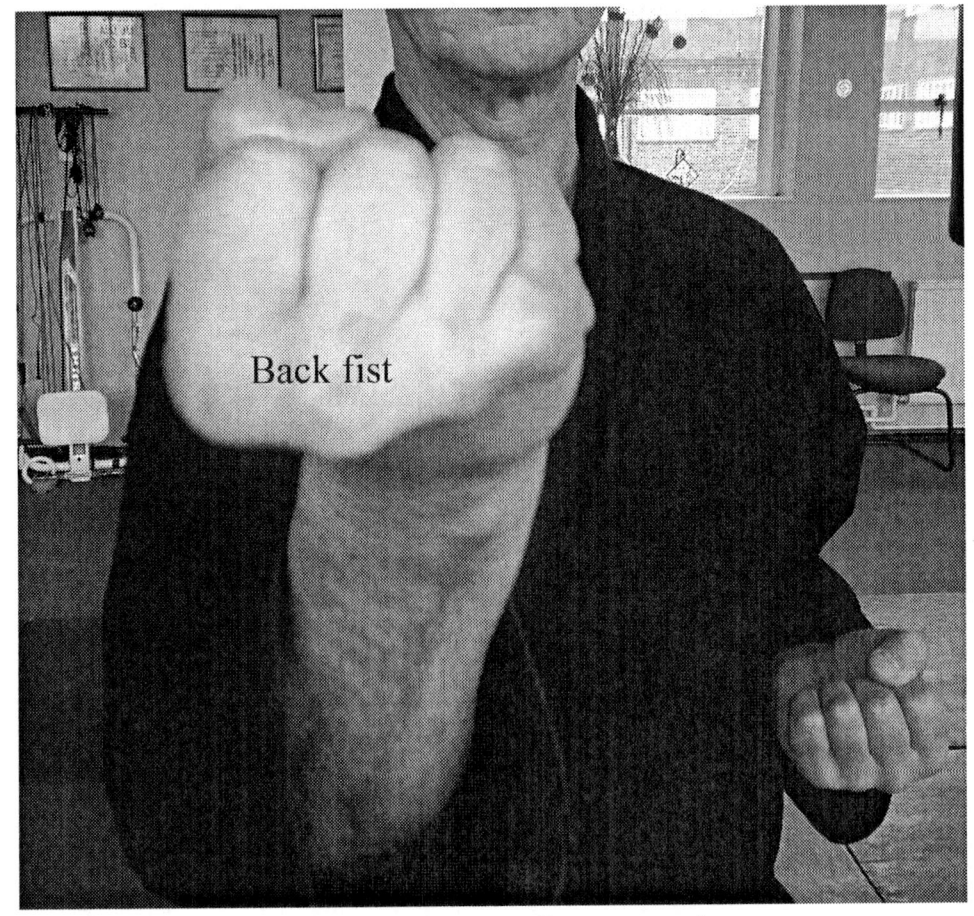

Back fist striking area. Illustration 39, b.

Back fist strikes are excellent for accurate and painful strikes to many areas of the body. For example, striking the breast bone with the back fist. This would cause immense pain. And a all time classic is using this technique to strike to the forehead. Preformed properly this would result in a knockout. Don't forget to practice both sided and add kiai to enhance the power of the strike.

Hammer Fist And Forward Stance

Stand in the ready position, bring the left leg forward in forward stance and raise the left arm up high to the left side at the same time bring the right arm across the waist line as shown in illustration 40, a.

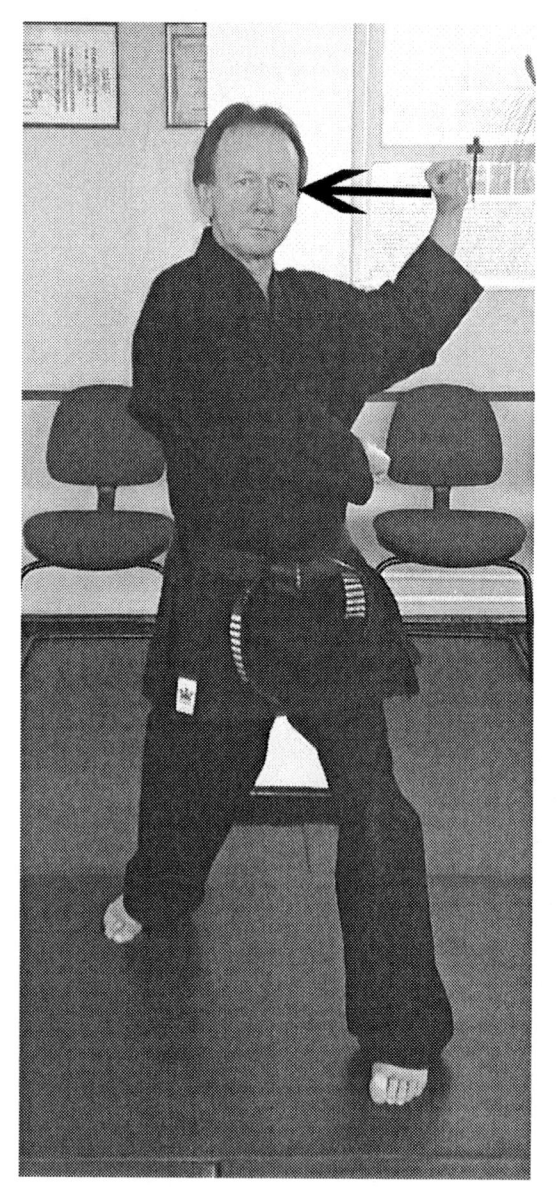

Starting the Hammer fist strike and forward stance. Illustration 40, a.

Completion of the hammer fist strike. Illustration 40, b.

Now pull the right hand back to the ready position and strike from left to right with the hammer fist hand as shown in illustration. As shown in illustration 40, b.

The hand area used for striking using the hammer fist is with the fist closed the fleshy and muscle area below the little finger. As shown in illustration 40, c. Be careful not to catch the little finger when practising this technique.

A Breath Of Fresh Air

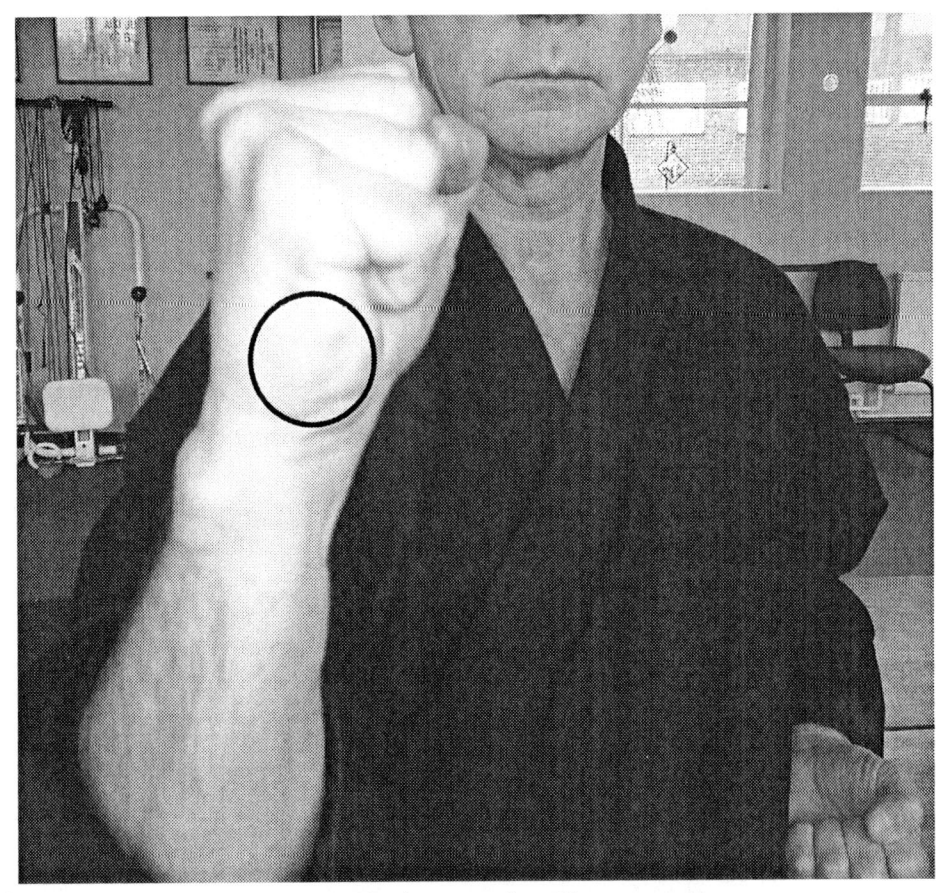

Striking area for hammer fist. Illustration 40, c.

The hammer fist strike is an extremely powerful and versatile strike. It can be used to strike any part of the body with atomic bomb like results. For more nuclear power add a kiai.

Palm Heel Strike And Forward Stance

Stand in the ready position; bring the right foot forward into forward stance. At the same time bring the left hand across the body and lift the right up to the right shoulder and opening the right hand. Relax the wrist. At the same time shift the body weight to the rear leg as shown in illustration. 41, a.

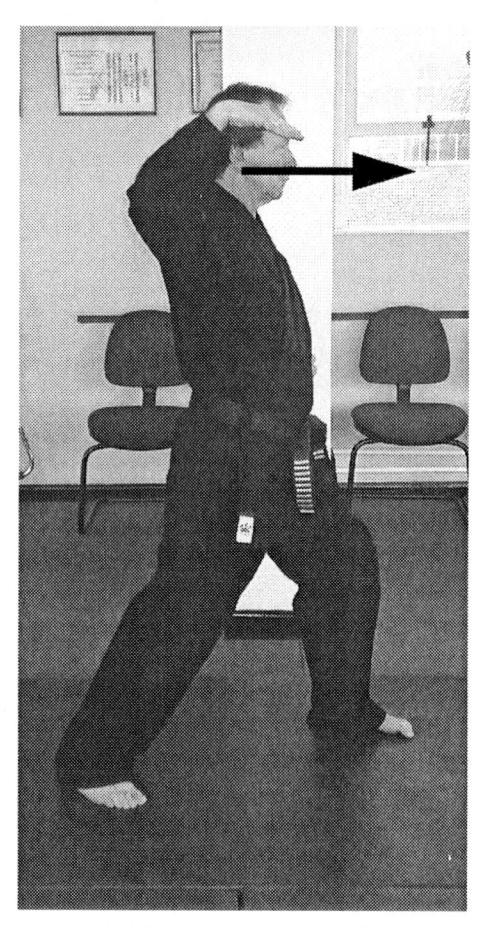

Starting the palm heel strike: and forward stance.
Illustration 41, a.

Palm heel strike and forward stance.
Illustration 41, b.

Now thrust the left hand forward locking the wrist as you do the strike and pull the right hand back to the prepared position. At the same time shift the body weight into forward stance. As shown in illustration 41, b. Note the bend in the elbow, this is to stop injury to the elbow joint. Locking the arm out straight will cause long term damage.

The area on the hand to strike with is the heel of the palm as shown in illustration 41, c.

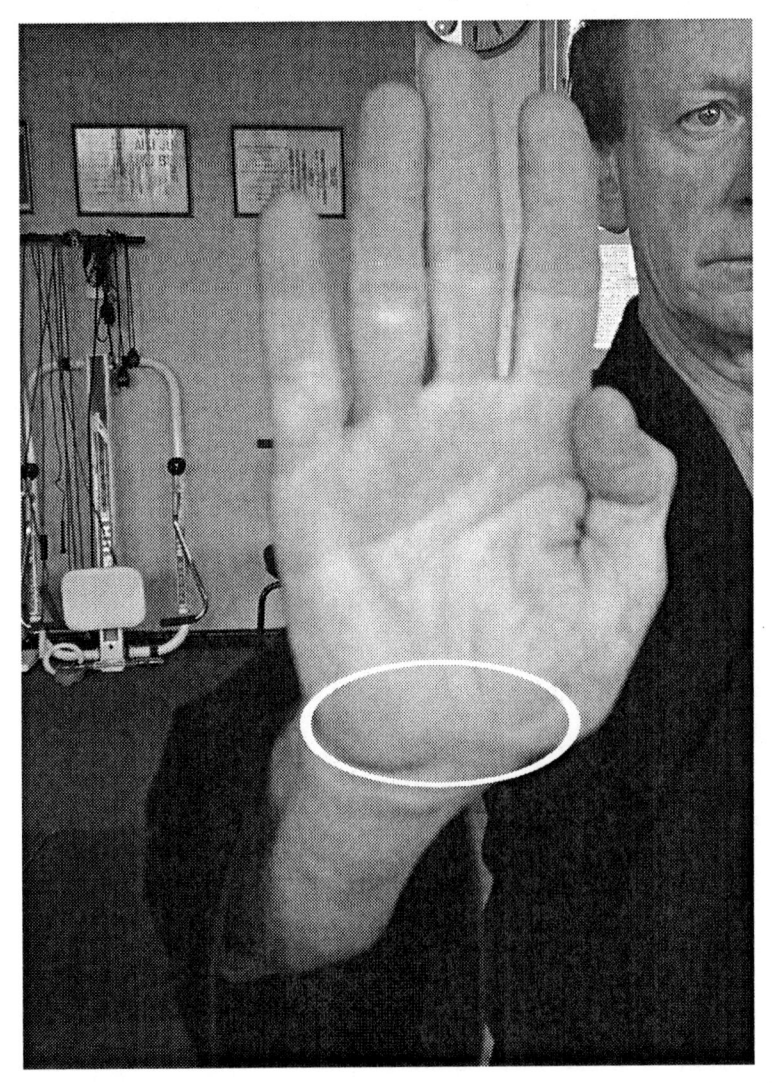

The thumb should be keep to the side of the hand, fingers slightly apart and straight. I have seen lots of karate styles do this technique bending the fingers from the second joint. This is a disaster if you actually land the strike, you would break all of the fingers on the striking hand.

The palm heel strike is one of the first flexible strikes I teach. Remember the karate kid film about painting the fences; well this is the real thing. To practice this flexible strikes start with light strikes. Stand in front of a partner with a suitable striking pad. Come into forward stance with the left leg forward. Raise the right hand fingers pointing forward as shown in illustration 41, a. As your hand travels toward the striking pad bend the wrist and pull the fingers so that the only part of the hand to hit the pad is the palm heel as shown in illustration 41,c. It will take practice to get this technique flowing but once you have the feel for it try doing it with the other hand. You can also add kiai to the technique for more power.

Front Kick Front Leg

Stand in fighting stance right leg forward. Raise the right leg up and bend the right knee, curling the toes upward as shown in illustration 42, a.

Starting the front leg front kick. Illustration 42, a.

Now thrust the right foot forward and kick with the ball of the foot as shown in illustration 42, b.

Front leg front kick. Illustration 42, b.

Return to fighting stance as soon as the kick is finished.

To help with balance, bend on the supporting leg and keep the hands up in the guard position.

The front leg front is a very fast kick. It is ideal for close quarter defences such as giving the attacker a swift kick in the groin.

Try doing this kick with the following foot variations, Kick with the ball of the foot, top of the foot and lower part of the shin, heel kick and axe kick

Kiai to enhance the power of the kicks and don't forget to practice them on both sides.

Close Quarter Side Kick

Stand in a fighting stance with the right shoulder touching the pad or punch bag as shown in illustration 43, a.

Illustration 43, a.   Illustration 43, b.

Step away from the pad with the left leg bending from the left knee having the toes pointing forward as shown in illustration 43, b.

Raise the right leg up bending from the right knee. At the same time drop the right arm down by your right side and raise the left on up to guard position as shown in illustration 43, c. The arm positioning helps with balance, another aid is to bend slightly on the knee of the supporting leg.

Illustration 43, c.   Illustration 43, d.

Now thrust the right leg backward, striking with the heel of the foot and kiai for power. Illustration 43, d shows the completion of the close quarter side kick.

Return to fighting stance immediately upon completion of the kick.

The close quarter side kick is exactly what it says it is, close quarter. If the attacker stands so close to you that your bodies are touching then this could be the one saves the day.

Practice the kick both side and try varying the height of the kick. Start with low shots and work upward. You can also try different foot positions such as, the edge of the foot and the ball of the foot. With all of these remember to put a kiai in to get more power.

Round House Kick Front Leg

Start with the right foot forward and stand in fighting stance. Raise the right leg up bending from the right knee at this point keep both hands up to help with your balance as shown in illustration 44, a.

Illustration 44, a.

Pivot at least forty five degrees on left foot and now thrust the right leg in an arc and strike the pad or punch bag with the top of the foot and lower part of the shin. As you thrust the right leg around, drop the right arm down by the right side as a counterbalance, as shown in illustration 44, b.

Front leg round house kick. Illustration 44, b.

Return to fighting stance immediately upon completion of the front leg round house kick.

The front leg round house kick is another fast powerful kick that works well in close quarter situations and is a cracker for taking out the thigh muscles. It will work equally as well on all other side areas of the body.

Try using the front leg round house kick with the ball of the foot; this will give you more kicking impact. You will need to change your angle of approach slightly so you do not catch the toes.

Once you have got the swing of this kick put in kiai to generate more power.

Turning Back Kick

Start in a fighting stance facing the target left leg forward as shown in illustration 45, a

Fighting stance. illustration 45, a.

The white arrow indicates the direction that you should step so that your back is pointing to the pad or bag.

A Breath Of Fresh Air

Step across parallel with left leg as shown in illustration 45, b. To gauge the distance of the step I would recommend about a shoulder width is reasonable.

Starting the turning back kick. Illustration 45, b.

Lift the left leg up towards your chest and bend the right knee, hands up in the counter balance position as shown in illustration 45, c.

Illustration 45, c.

Now thrust the right leg back striking with the heel and keep the arms up to help with counter balance as shown in illustration 45, c.

Completion of the turning back kick. Illustration 45, d.

Return to fighting stance immediately after the completion of the turning back kick.

I have mentioned this earlier in this book but it is worth covering this again. Always look to the side that you are about to kick, that is to say if you are going to kick with the right leg look over the right shoulder and if you are going to kick with the left leg look over the left shoulder. Never look one way and kick the opposite way, this is extremely bad and could cause serious lower back injuries. I would not hesitate to say that this kind of injury is an orthopaedic surgeon's nightmare.

The purpose of a turning or spinning technique is that it adds rotational force to the movement and this gives the kick more power. In the mid seventies full contact karate tournaments were the in thing and a guy nick named "Benny the Jet" became world famous for pulling of the turning back kick with rib cracking results.

Once you have got to grips with the turning kick on one side turn your attention to the other side and add kiai for more "Jet" power.

Turning Round House Kick

Start by standing in fighting stance left leg forward facing the bag or pad. As shown in illustration 46, a

Fighting stance Illustration 46, a.

Step about a shoulders width across parallel, as shown in illustration in 46, b.

Starting the turning round house kick. illustration 46, b.

Lift the right leg up and swing it in an arc backwards towards the target striking with the heel of the right foot, at the same time drop the right arm to the right side and use the left arm to assist in counter balancing. As shown in illustration 47, c.

Completion of the turning round house kick. Illustration 47, b.

Return to fighting stance as soon as the kick is finished.

What a dynamite kick, the turning round house kick is, it generates lots of power by using rotational force and if landed in the right spot will easily blow the strongest opponent away quickly. To make this kick even more explosive add kiai.

This kick is so much fun that I bet you have done it both sides without me having to mention it.

Now that I have demonstrated a few more blocks, strikes and kicking techniques it is time to put some of these into practise. To do this I will show some more defence routines. In chapter one I explained the distance rule but this is the real world and it is not always possible to keep your distance.

Lapel Hold And Downward Blow

In this first defence routine the attacker has taken a hold of the lapel with his left hand and has raised the right hand up indicating his intention to strike me, an attack like this would probably done with a weapon in the attacker's hand. I have already come into fighting stance and have my hands up ready to deal with the attack as shown in illustration 48, a

Attacker grabs my lapel. Illustration 48, a.

The attacker then proceeds to attempt strike with a downward blow to my head. Immediately move forward on the left leg and go into forward stance. At the same time stop the attackers arm by applying the rising cross block. As shown in illustration 48, b. Kiai when you do the rising cross block.

Applying the rising cross block. Illustration 48, b.

Have your right arm on top of the left for the rising cross block and stop the downward blow before the attacker right arm passes his right shoulder. If you do not stop the attacking blow quickly the blow will have more power and you will have to work harder.

Raise the right leg up and bend from the knee, as you do this, thrust the knee forward so you knee kick the attacker in the solar plexus or groin, which ever you can reach. As shown in illustration 48, c: Kiai when you do the knee kick.

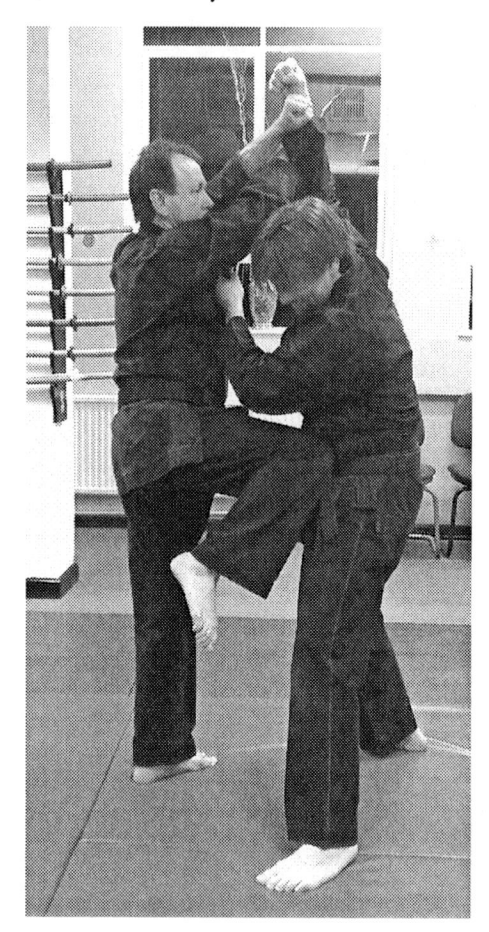

Delivering a knee kick. Illustration 48, c.   Illustration 48, d.

Now drop the attacker's right arm down and at the same time put your right foot back on the floor as shown in illustration 48, d.

As soon as you drop the attackers arm swing the arm across your body from left to right. Have your left arm under the attacker's right and reach with left hand towards the attacker's right wrist. An elbow lock should just be starting to come on. As shown in illustration 48, e.

Illustration 48, e.

James Moclair

Lift the attacker arm up higher and draw the attackers arm out completely straight and apply an elbow lock by lifting up with your left arm which is under the attacker elbow joint. The right hand should twist the attacker wrist toward you to enhance the lock as shown in illustration 48, f.

Illustration 48, f.

Illustration 48, f, a shows a close shot of the elbow lock and correct hand positions.

Release the elbow lock and use the left hand to drive the attacker's right arm down towards his groin area. At the same time draw the right hand back ready to deliver a strike. As shown in illustration 48, g.

Illustration 48, g.

Finishing the routine, with a reverse punch
Illustration 48, h.

Finish of the routine by doing a reverse punch with the right fist to the jaw of the attacker, as shown in illustration 48, h. Kiai when you do the reverse punch.

Return to fighting stance immediately after finishing the reverse punch.

Lapel Hold And Side Blow

For the next attack, the attacker takes a hold on the lapel with the left hand and then attempts to throw a punch to the side of my head with the right hand as shown in illustration 49, a.

Attacker about the throw a side blow. Illustration 49, a.

Next the attacker fires the blow towards the head. Advance forward into forward stance and at the same time block using a re-enforced outside forearm block. To do the re-enforced outside forearm block place the right hand palm heel onto the left arm as you are doing the outside forearm block. This blocking method gives tremendous blocking power and is ideally suited for close quarter work. As shown in illustration 49, b. Kiai when you do the re-enforced outside forearm block.

Applying a re-enforced outside forearm block. Illustration 49, b.

Stop the attacker blow before his hand passes his shoulder so that it does not gain too much power.

Now grasp the attacker right hand with your left hand and at the same time deliver an elbow strike to the side of the attackers face or neck with the right arm as shown in illustration 49, c.

Elbow strike to face or neck. Illustration 49, c.

James Moclair

With your right arm take it around the attackers head and place your forearm across the attacker throat. The attacker head should now be under the right arm pit. The left hand lets go of the attacker's right arm and takes hold of your own right hand. Step back further with the right leg so that the attacker is up on his toes and apply upward force with the right arm. This will apply a strangulation to the attacker throat. As shown in illustration 49, d.

Applying a strangulation. Illustration 49, d.

Extreme care should be taken when applying any neck lock or strangulation. They are extremely effective techniques, ease the neck lock or strangulation on. Never bang these techniques on with full force. It could prove fatal.

Lift the attackers head up with the right left hand, palm facing up and fingers gripping the wind pipe. At the same time draw your right hand back ready to strike as shown in illustration 49, e.

Illustration 49, e.

Finally to complete this routine do a reverse punch to the attacker chin as shown in illustration 49, f. Kiai on the reverse punch.

Reverse punch to finish the routine. Illustration 49, f.

Return to fighting stance immediately upon completion of the reverse punch.

Lapel Hold And Straight Punch To The Face

As before the attacker has taken a grip of the lapel but this time his intention is to do a straight punch to the face as shown in illustration 50, a

Illustration 50, a.

As the attacker throws the punch with his right hand, quarter step to his right out side. At the same time block the punch with an outside forearm block as shown in illustration 50, b.

Illustration 50, b.

Quickly pass your right arm up under the attacker right arm and reach up so you're inside forearm makes contact with the side of the attacker's neck. At the same time have your left arm reach up and clasp both hands together palm to palm. With your head tucked in apply pressure by pulling the attacker towards you. This will apply a side neck lock as shown in illustration 50, c.

Applying a side neck lock. Illustration 50, c.

Extreme care should be taken when applying any neck lock or strangulation. They are extremely effective techniques, ease the neck lock or strangulation on. Never bang these techniques on with full force. In this particular technique it would be very easy to knock your training partner out with just a little too much force.

With the right knee, knee kick the attacker in the solar plexus or groin, which ever you can reach. Kiai with the knee kick. At the same time let go with the left hand. As shown in illustration 50, d.

Knee kick the attacker. Illustration 50, d.

As you finish the knee kick step back with the right foot pulling the attacker forward and deliver a palm heel strike to the nape of neck with your right hand. As shown in illustration 50, e.

Palm heel strike to the nap of the neck. Illustration 50, e.

Continue the palm heel strike all the way through and drive the attacker to the floor as shown in illustration 50, f.

Driving the attacker to the floor with the palm heel strike. Illustration 50, f.

Finish of the routine by doing a heel kick to the coccyx (Base of the spine) with the right foot as shown in illustration 50, g. Kiai on the heel kick.

Kick to the attacker's coccyx. Illustration 50, g.

Return to fighting stance immediately after the heel kick.

Hands Restrained From The Front

In the next attack, the attacker grasps both hands from the front. Immediately get into posture by stepping back with the right leg. As shown in illustration 51, a.

Attacker grasps both hands. Illustration 51, a.

Step back on left leg, this will allow you to move your hands. Raise your left hand up, palm facing towards you. At the same time grasp hold of the attacker's right hand with your right hand. The fingers of your right hand should be into the palm of the attacker hand and your thumb should be placed on the back of the attackers hand as shown in illustration 51, b. Also shown in the close shot illustration 51, b, a.

Illustration 51, b.

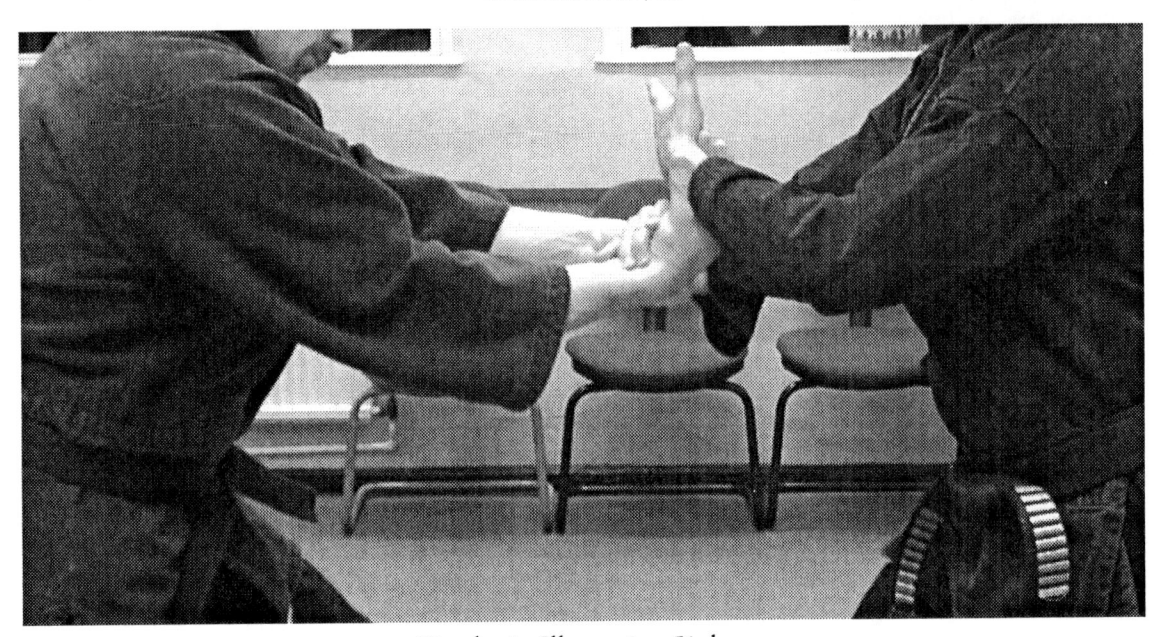

Hand grip Illustration 51, b, a.

Now deliver a front leg front kick using the top of the foot to the attackers groin as shown in illustration 51, c. Kiai with the kick.

James Moclair

Kick the attacker in the groin. Illustration 51, c.

From the kick to the groin step back as far as you can with the right foot, do this in a smooth motion. As shown in illustration 51,c, a.

Illustration 51,c,a.

Draw the attacker to the floor by placing both hands on the attacker's right hand. Both the right and left fingers should be grasping into the palm of the attackers right hand and both thumbs should be on the back of the attacker's right hand. This should put a wrist lock on the attacker's right wrist. As shown in illustration 51, d and also the close shot in illustration 51, d, a.

Illustration 51, d.

Make sure that the attackers elbow is on the floor, this will ensure a powerful wrist lock. It is quite normal when drawing the attacker to the floor that they sometimes land face down as opposed to landing on their back. Either way the lock works well so don't get in a flap if it happens while you are trying this technique.

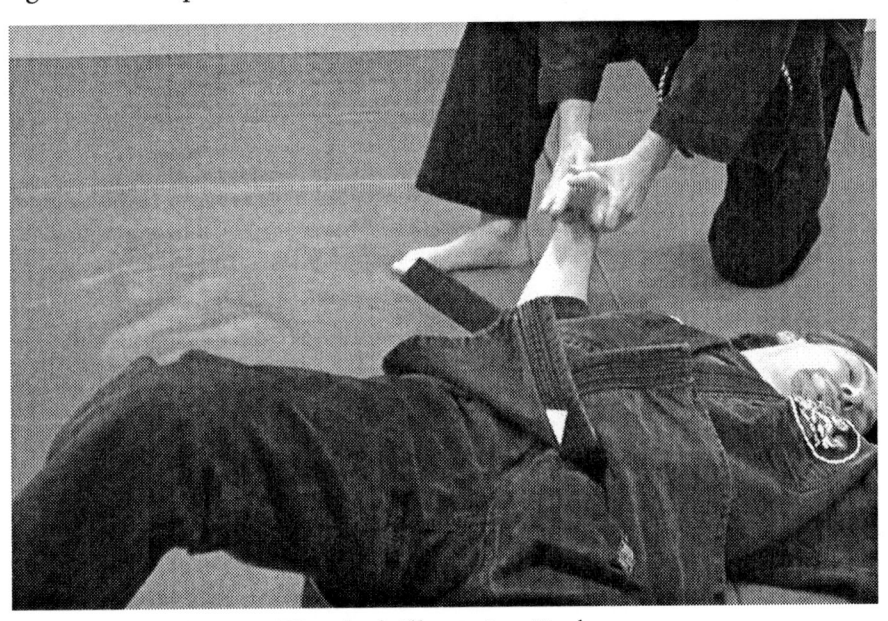

Wrist lock Illustration 51, d, a.

James Moclair

To finish of the routine, let go of the attacker's hand and come into a standing position. As soon as you are standing; strike to the attackers solar plexus with a right heel kick, as shown in illustration 51, e. Kiai on the kick.

Heel kicking: to the attacker's solar plexus. Illustration 51, e.

Return to fighting stance immediately after the heel kick.

Hands Restrained From The Rear

For the next attack the attacker has come from the rear and grasped both hands as shown in illustration 52, a

Hands restrained from the rear. Illustration 52, a

James Moclair

Step back with your right leg into straddle stance and right elbow strike the attackers chin as shown in illustration 52, b. My left hand has taken a hold of the attackers left wrist, so that you can see this I have had to turn around for the next photograph.

Elbow the attacker under his chin. Illustration 52, b.

Illustration 52, c shows the hand grip that is described in the previous illustration

The white arrow indicates the direction that you need to pull to draw the attacker of balance.

Hand grip Illustration 52, c

Continue to drive the attacker back with the elbow strike at the same time pull with your right hand so that he is completely of balance as shown in illustration 52, d

Illustration 52, d.

The action will drive the attacker backward to the ground. Keep a hold on the attacker left wrist as shown in illustration 52, e.

Illustration 52, e.

James Moclair

Now turn around so that you are facing the attacker with your left leg forward as shown in illustration 52, f.

Illustration 52, f.

To finish off this routine deliver a front angled kick to the attackers elbow and pull back with your right hand to apply a lock or given enough force the two actions could break the attackers arm as shown in illustration 52, g. Kiai with the front angled kick

Illustration 52, g.

Return to fighting stance immediately after finishing the front angled kick.

Single Lapel Hold

In the next attack the attacker grasps the lapel with the left hand. This time the technique will take him down before he has a chance to strike with the free hand. Start, by immediately taking posture: with the left leg forward as shown in illustration 53, a.

Illustration 53, a.

Reach immediately across with the right hand and grasp the attacker's right arm above the elbow at the back of the tricep muscle. At the same time move the left leg forward so that you are in forward stance as shown in illustration 53, b.

Illustration 53, b.

James Moclair

Now pull the arm from your left to your right. At the same time step with your left leg past the attackers right side and reach with the left hand and place it on the attackers face with the fingers on the right side and low by the chin as shown in illustration 53, c.

Illustration 53, c.

Pull the left hand across so that it turns the attacker head to his right side as shown in illustration 53, c. At the same time reverse back on the left leg and start to draw the attacker further of balance as shown in illustration

Illustration 53, c.

Continue to draw the attacker of balance and throw him to the floor by reversing the left foot 180 degrees and still keep a hold on the attacker's right arm. As shown in illustration 53, e.

Illustration 53, e.

With the left hand draw the elbow joint of the attacker arm across the top of your left shin and pull back. This will apply a powerful elbow lock. As you apply the elbow lock drop your left knee in to the attacker's rib cage to assist in body control. As shown in illustration 53, f.

Illustration 53, f.

James Moclair

To conclude this routine, with your right hand deliver a punch to the rig cage of the attacker still keeping the elbow lock and knee in place as shown in illustration 53, g. Kiai with the punch.

Strike to the rib cage finish routine. Illustration 53, g.

Once you have finished the punch to the ribs, return to fighting stance.

Both Lapels Held

For the next defence routine the attacker has taken hold of both lapels, while this on the surface does not seem like a bad attack you have to be aware of the possibility of him trying to head butt or knee kick you. Illustration 54, a, shows the initial attack.

The attacker has taken a hold of both lapels. Illustration 54, a.

James Moclair

Use the right hand arc fist to strike to the attacker groin. As you do the arc fist strike step forward with the right leg into a straddle stance. As shown in illustration 54, b. and 54, b, a.

Use the arc fist to strike the attackers groin. Illustration 54, b.

As the strike to the groin will make the attacker drop his head, keep your head to one side so you do not accidentally get struck with a head butt.

Illustration 54, b, a.

Bring the right arm to the top of the attacker's right thigh as shown in illustration 54, c.

Illustration 54, c.

With your left hand reach down and take a hold of the back of the attacker's right leg. As shown in illustration 54, d.

Illustration 54, d.

Push with your right arm and pull with the left to throw the attacker to the floor as shown in illustration 54, d.

Throw the attacker to the floor. Illustration 54, d.

Keep a hold of the attacker's right leg and advance forward so you position yourself in between the attacker's legs. And give him the good news with a right heel kick to the solar plexus. As shown in illustration 54, d.

Illustration 54, d.

To conclude this routine, throw the attackers right leg to his left shoulder to turn him onto his side as shown in illustration 54, d and 54, d ,a.

Illustration 54, d.

Illustration 54, d, a.

Return to a fighting stance to finish this routine.

Pull Back On The Shoulder From The Rear

The attacker has come from the rear and has grabbed my left shoulder. His intention is to pull me to the floor as shown in illustration 55, a.

Attacker initialising the attack by grabbing my shoulder. Illustration 55, a.

To maintain balance you must step back immediately with the left leg. At the same time, strike with the right hand using the back of your hand, hitting the attacker on the side of his face as shown in illustration 55, b. Kiai on the strike to the face.

Illustration 55, b.

The white arrow on the illustration 55, b indicates the direction you need to step back with in order to maintain your balance.

After striking the attackers face, continue in a smooth motion to wrap your left arm around the attacker's right arm as shown in illustration 55, c. This should start to apply an elbow lock.

Starting to apply an elbow lock. Illustration 55, c.

Keep the arm lock on with your left arm, use the right hand to grip the attacker's throat. It is important to keep the right arm straight as this contributes to breaking the attackers balance. As shown in illustration 55, d.

Illustration 55, d

Step past the attacker with the right leg and drive him to the floor. As you throw the attacker to the floor, keep the elbow lock and move the right hand away from the attacker's throat and slide so it rests on the attacker's right shoulder. Now get your left hand to grasp your right arm and pull upwards, this will apply a powerful lock as shown in illustration 55, e.

Illustration 55, e.

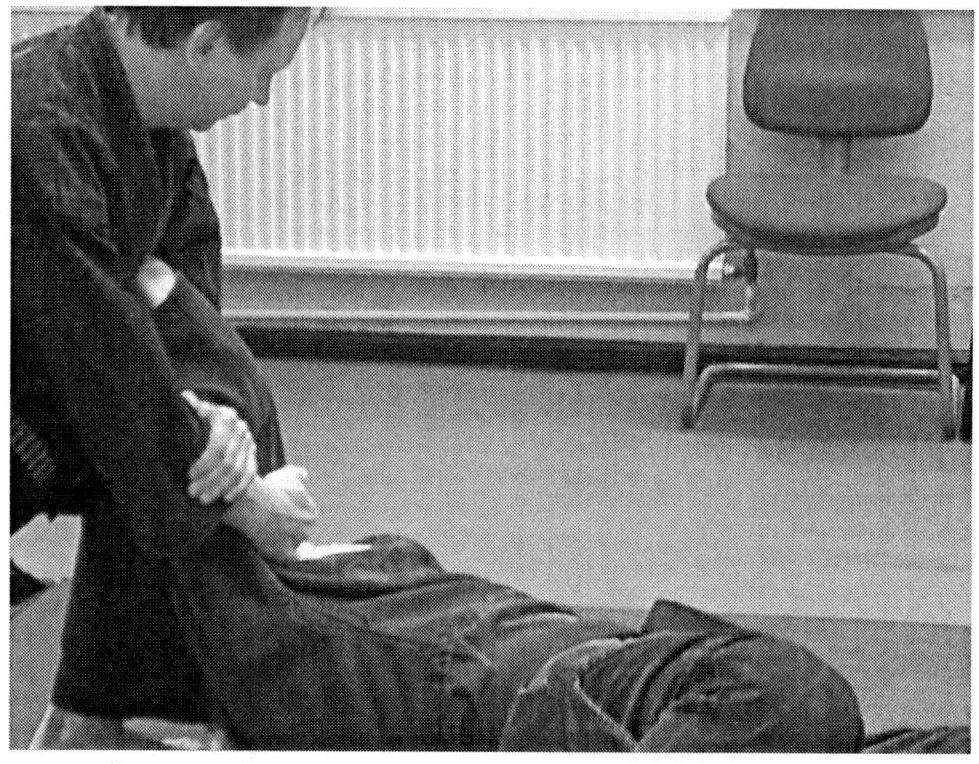

Illustration 55,e,a. is a close up of the hand positions for the elbow lock

To finish the routine, let go of the lock and deliver a strike to the rib cage with your right hand as shown in illustration 55, f. Kiai with the punch.

Punch to the rib cage Illustration 55. f.

Return to fighting stance immediately after striking the attacker's rib cage.

Pull Back On The Shoulder And Side Blow The Face

In the next attack the attacker starts by coming from the rear and takes a hold of my jacket at the shoulder with his right hand, as shown in illustration 56, a.

Illustration 56, a.

The attacker pulls back sharply with his right hand and then swings a blow to my head with his left hand. In order to maintain my balance from the pull I have stepped back with my right leg and come into forward stance. At the same time I have blocked the incoming blow with a reverse outside forearm block. I have also raised my left arm up and struck the attacker right arm again with an outside forearm block. Both blocks are done together and with equal power. As shown in illustration 56, b.

Blocking the side blow and striking the attackers right arm. Illustration 56, b.

With the left hand take hold of the attacker's right arm. At the same time with the right leg deliver shin kick to the inner thigh of the attacker's right leg. The right hand has to reach across and grabs the attackers right arm also and with both hands lift his right arm up. The left hand goes on top and the right hand goes underneath as shown in illustration 56,c.

Illustration 56, c

It is tempting to kick the attacker in the groin, but don't. It will only make him drop to his knees and you will loose the next part of the technique.

After delivering the shin kick put the right foot down and drop the attackers left arm down. As shown in illustration 56, d.

Illustration 56, d.

James Moclair

Continue to swing the attackers arm up in an arc and place your left arm underneath the attackers elbow gripping his wrist with your left and right hands. This will now apply a powerful elbow lock. As shown in illustration 56, e and also 56, e, a.

Illustration 56, e.

Elbow lock Illustration 56, e, a

Draw your right hand back to preparation position and at the same time with the left hand push the attacker's right hand away from you as shown in illustration 56, f.

Illustration 56, f.

To conclude the routine, finish with a reverse punch to the chin. As shown in illustration 54, g. Kiai with the punch.

Illustration 56, g.

Return to fighting stance after completing the reverse punch.

Pull On The Sleeve From The Rear

The next routine has the attacker grabbing a hold of my left of sleeve from the rear with his right hand. As shown in illustration 57, a.

Pull on the sleeve from rear. Illustration 57, a.

As the attacker tries to pull you backward, step back with your right leg so that you maintain your balance. At the same time grab hold of the attacker wrist with your left wrist with your left hand, as shown in illustration 57, b.

Illustration 57, b.

The white arrow in illustration 57, b indicates the direction that you need to step back in, in order to keep your balance.

In one smooth motion, step past the attacker with the right leg and hit him under the chin with your right forearm. At the same time pull the attacker right arm to your left side to unbalance him as shown in illustration 57, c.

Illustration 57, c.

Continue driving through until the attacker hit the floor as shown in illustration 57, d

Illustration 57, d.

To finish the routine, do a heel kick to the attacker's rib cage as shown in illustration 57, c. Remember to kiai with the heel kick.

Heel kick to ribs. Illustration 57, c.

Return to fighting stance as soon as you complete the heel kick.

Pull On Wrist From The Rear With A Side Blow

The next attack comes, with the attacker coming from the rear and grabbing my left wrist and pulling me back, at the same time with his right hand he throws a punch to my face. As in the previous routine you must step back to keep your balance, at the same time you have to deal with the blow to the face by blocking this with a reverse outside forearm block with the right arm. As you block use the left hand to grab hold of the attackers right wrist as shown in illustration 58, a.

Attacker grabs wrist from rear and throws a punch to the head Illustration 58, a.

With the right elbow, elbow strike the attacker under his chin and at the same time pull the attackers right arm to your right side to break his balance as shown in illustration 58 , b.

Illustration 58, b.

Follow through with the elbow strike and keep pulling on the attacker's right arm until he falls to the floor. When he hits the floor keep a hold of the attacker's right hand as shown in illustration 58, c.

Illustration 58, c.

A Breath Of Fresh Air

While holding onto the attackers right arm, apply an elbow lock, by placing the attackers elbow joint on the top of your shin and then pulling back as shown in illustration 58 , d and close up illustration 58, d, a.

Elbow lock with the shin. Illustration 58, d

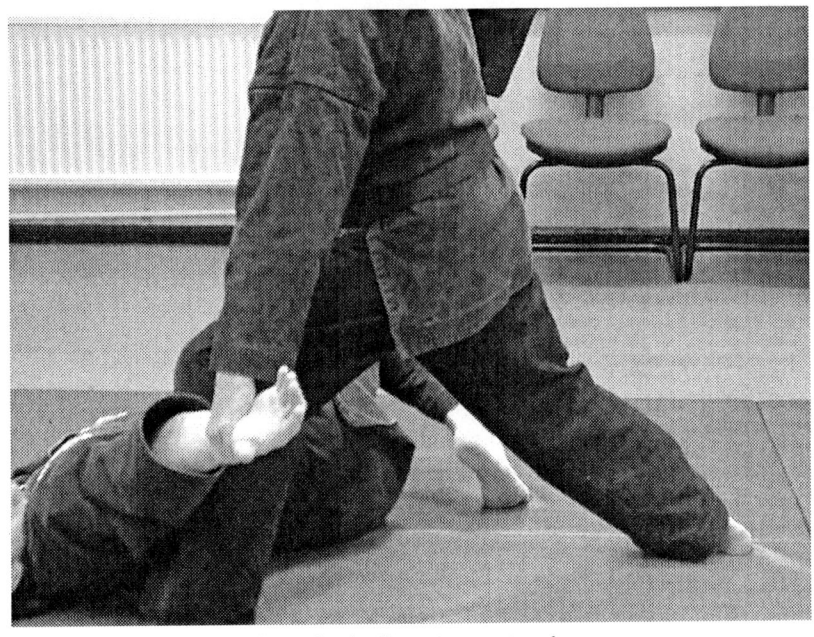

Elbow lock Illustration 58, d, a.

To finalise this routine, keep a hold of the attacker's right arm and heel kick the attacker in the ribs as shown in illustration 58, e. Kiai on the heel kick.

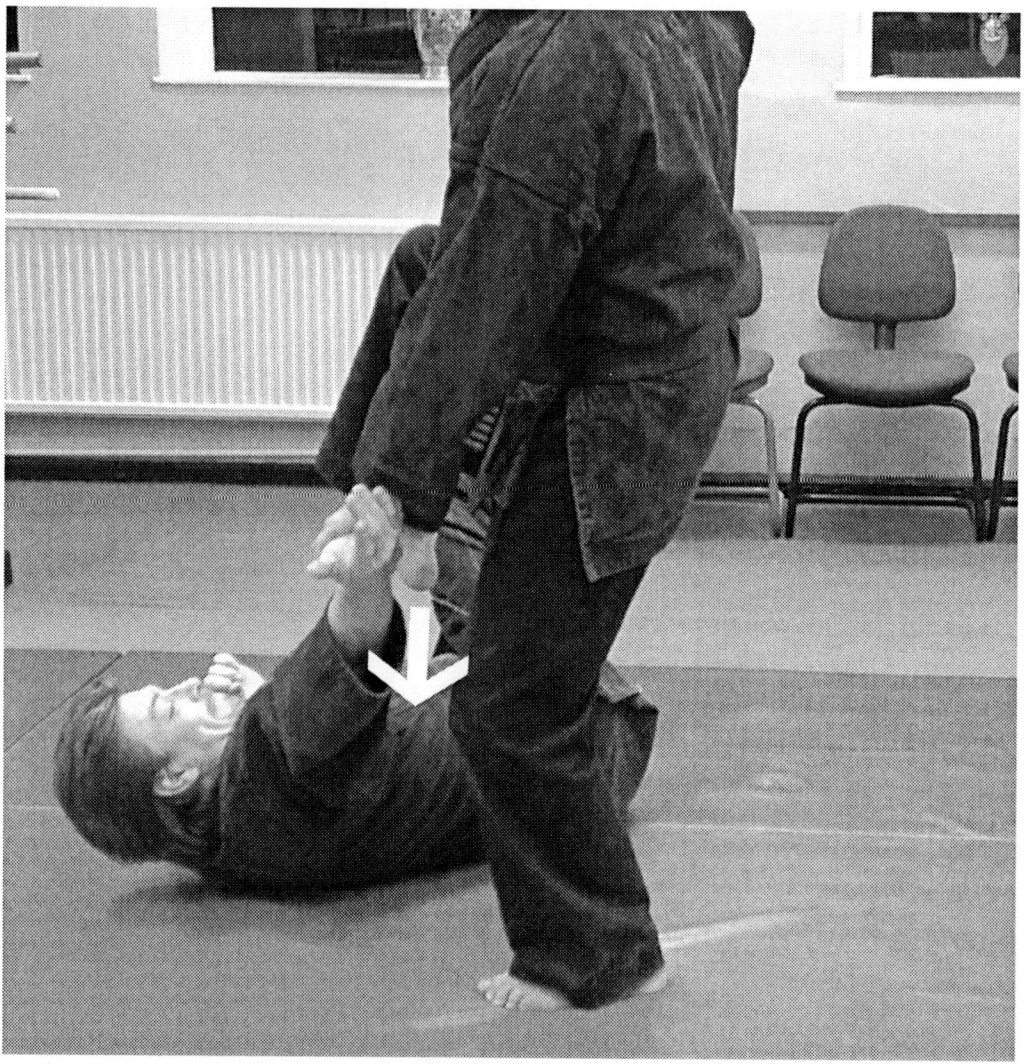

Return to fighting stance immediately after doing the heel kick.

This concludes the white belt to yellow belt syllabus. In the next chapter I will include the techniques for yellow belt to orange belt.

The Beginning Of The Orange Belt Syllabus

The first of the blocking techniques is a flexible arc fist block: that is to say that the hand is open and relaxed when blocking the attack. While this may seem on the surface not as powerful as the block striking it is indeed just as powerful if not a little more painful. By having the hand open and the arm muscles relaxed you can generate a lot more speed and speed equals velocity, this in turn gives the block power. The flexible block is again done on the same basis as the block strike and you attack the arm by powering through the attackers arm.

Arc Fist Bock

The arc fist block is preformed by standing in the ready position, and then stepping forward with the left leg. As you are stepping forward bring the right arm over the left, and open the left hand as shown in illustration 59, a.

Illustration 59, a.   Illustration 59, b.

Pull the right hand to your right hip in preparation position and with the wrist relaxed thrust the left hand out as shown in illustration 59, b and also 59, b, a.

James Moclair

When doing the arc fist block the hand does not make any contact. The striking area is just below the wrist joint. As shown in illustration 59, b, a.

Arc fist block contact point

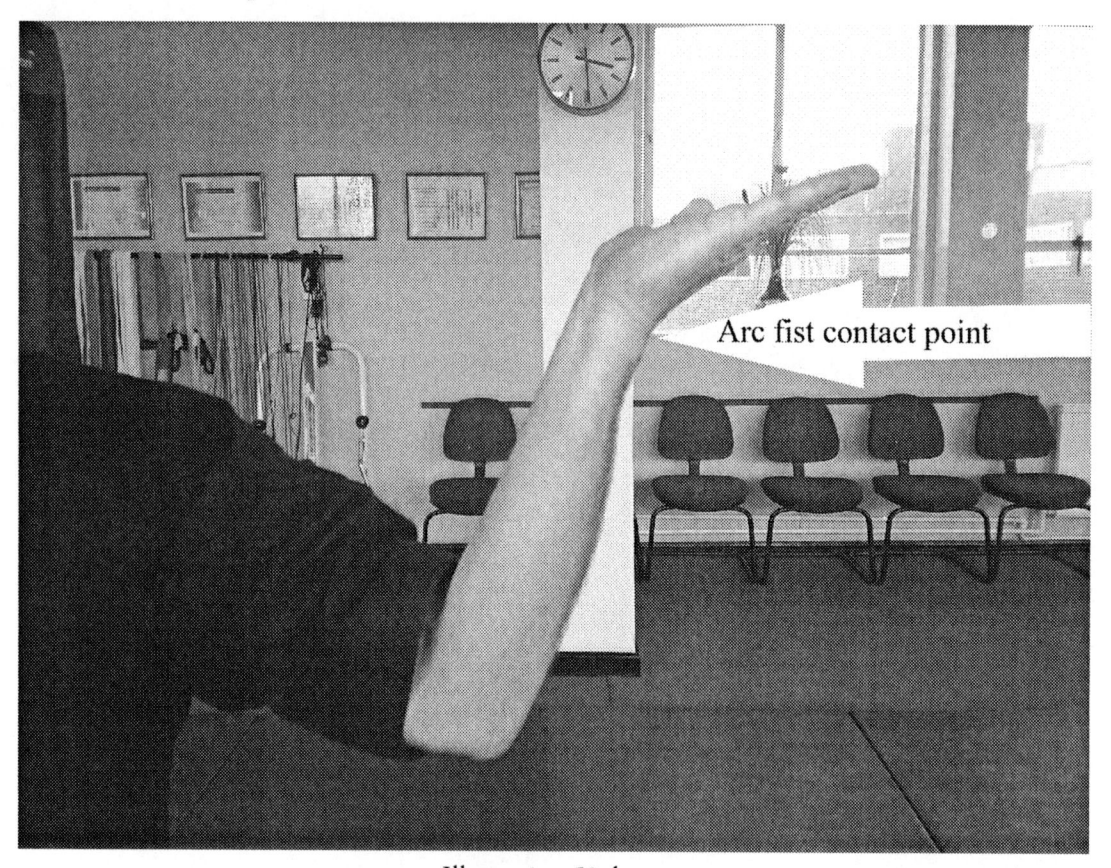

Illustration 59, b, a.

Ridge Hand Strike

The ridge hand strike is an excellent all round striking method but it takes practice. It is also a good technique to use after performing the arc fist block.

Stand in the ready position, and step forward with the left leg, at the same time bring the left arm across your chest and drop the right arm down by your right side and also open your right hand as shown in illustration 60, a.

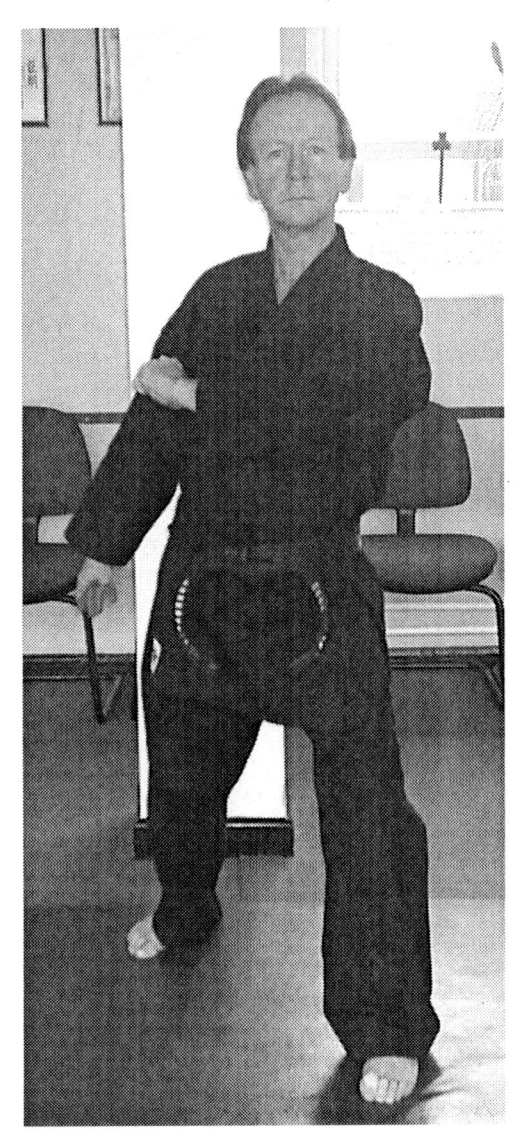

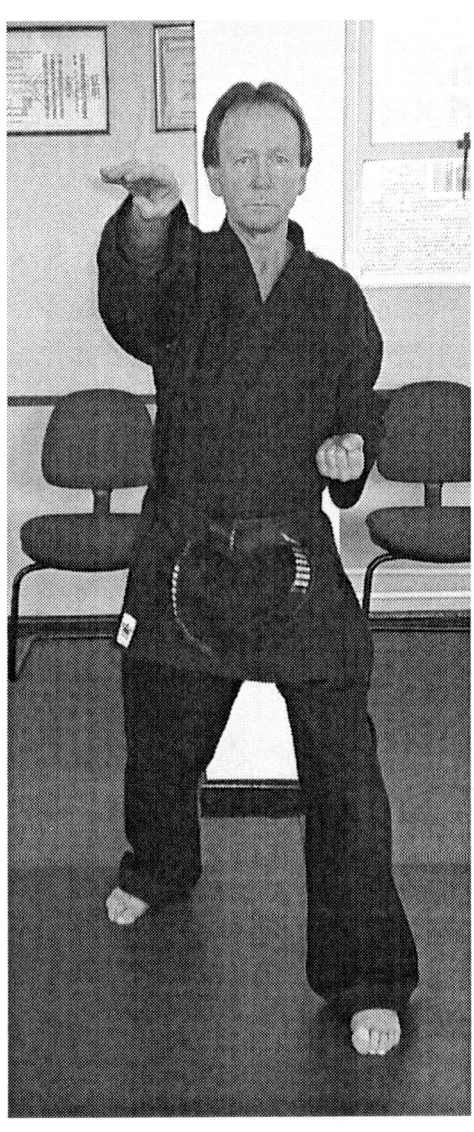

Illustration 60, a.　　　　Illustration 60, b.

Pull the right hand back to the preparation position and strike out with the ridge of the hand as shown in illustration 60, b.

To practice the ridge hand strike, point your thumb to the little finger and have your fingers pointing away from you. The hand should be tilted a fraction towards you as shown in illustration 60, c. The oval shape on my hand in illustration 60,c is the striking area for the ridge hand strike.

James Moclair

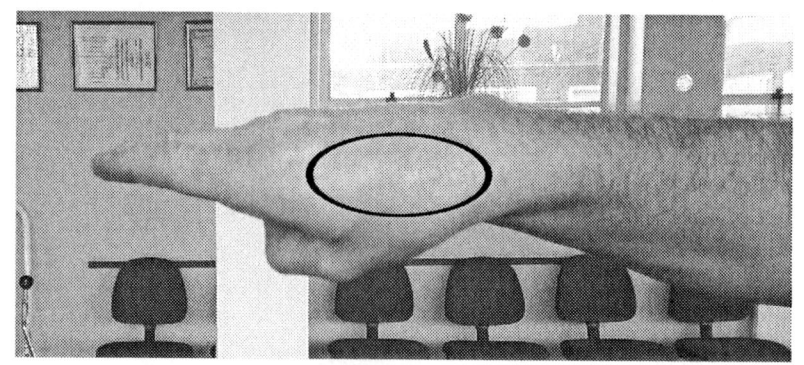

Illustration 60, c.

Elbow Block

The elbow block and arm trap is used for extremely close quarter punches to the head.

Start by standing in the ready position. Step forward with the left leg and at the same time bring the left arm across your body, have the elbow higher than your hand. The right hand is pulled back to the hip in preparation position as shown in illustration 61, a.

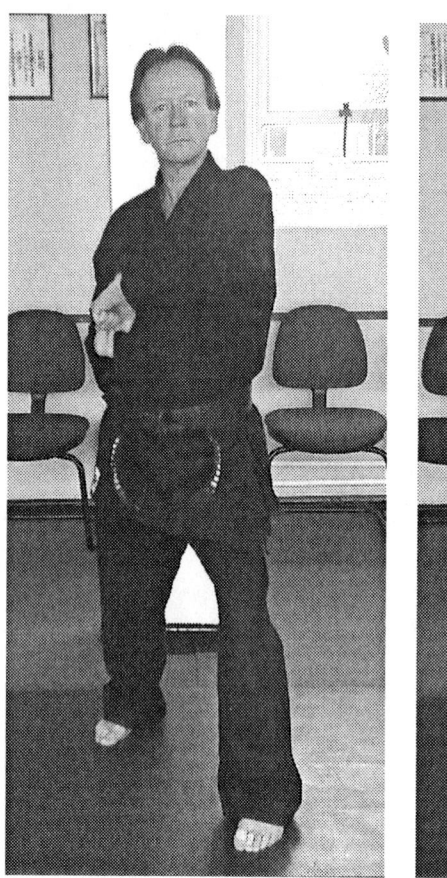

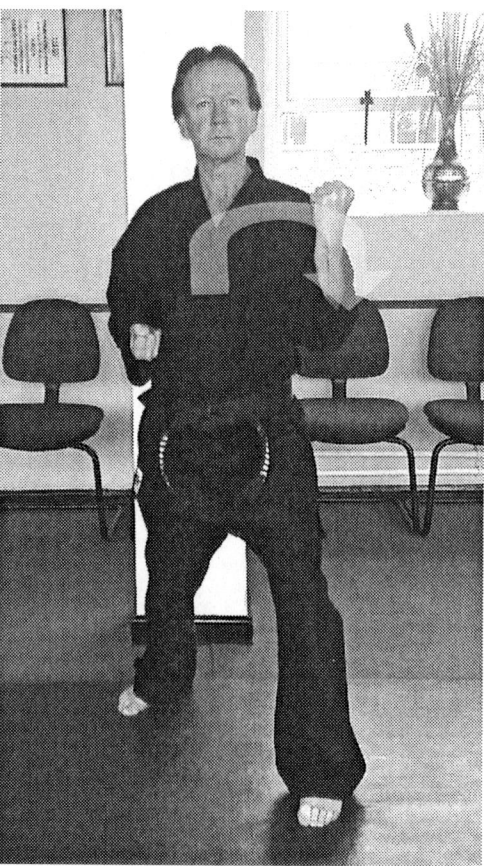

Illustration 61, a   Illustration 61, b.

Swing the left arm in a big arc so that you end up with the elbow by your left hip and the left hand pointing upward as shown in illustration 61, b.

Upper Cut

Illustration 62, a.

Illustration 62, b.

To compliment the elbow block: an upper cut is the ideal knockout strike, start by standing in the ready position. Step forward with the left leg into forward stance and pull the right hand back into preparation position at the same time bring the left arm across your body with the left hand by your right side as shown in illustration 62, a.

From the right hip launch the right hand up in a straight line up the centre of your body, at the same time pull the left hand back to the left hip in preparation position as shown in illustration 62, b.

The first two knuckles on your fist are the contact points and to achieve a sensational knockout hit the attacker directly under the chin. Remember to kiai.

Round House Punch

Another sensational strike is the round house punch. Start by standing in the ready position, step forward with your left leg and pull the right hand back into preparation position at the same time bring the right arm across the body so that the right hand is by your right side as shown in illustration 63, a.

Illustration 63, a   Illustration 63, b.

Now with the right hand, punch so that the hand travels from right to left and just above your shoulder height. The left hand is pulled back to the left hip in preparation position as shown in illustration 63 b.

You can use the round house punch to strike the side of the attacker face but if you want a nice little jaw breaker than hit the jaw bone at the point that allows the jaw to open and close. Ouch

A Breath Of Fresh Air

Wall Fighting Stance

For the first of the defence in this section I have chosen to start with a defence where you are pushed against a wall or similar surface. Your posture is vital to ensure you can start a safe line of defence. I have developed what I call "Wall Posture Position" for this type of attack. To practice this, stand with your back to a wall, bring the left leg forward and turn your knees inward to protect the groin area. Have the right heel of the right foot tightly against the base of the wall for stability. Your buttocks should be touching the wall and only the spine of your back should make contact, therefore you need to round your back of in order to achieve this. Tilt you head forward so it does not make contact with the wall and tense the neck muscles up. As shown in illustration 64, a and b.

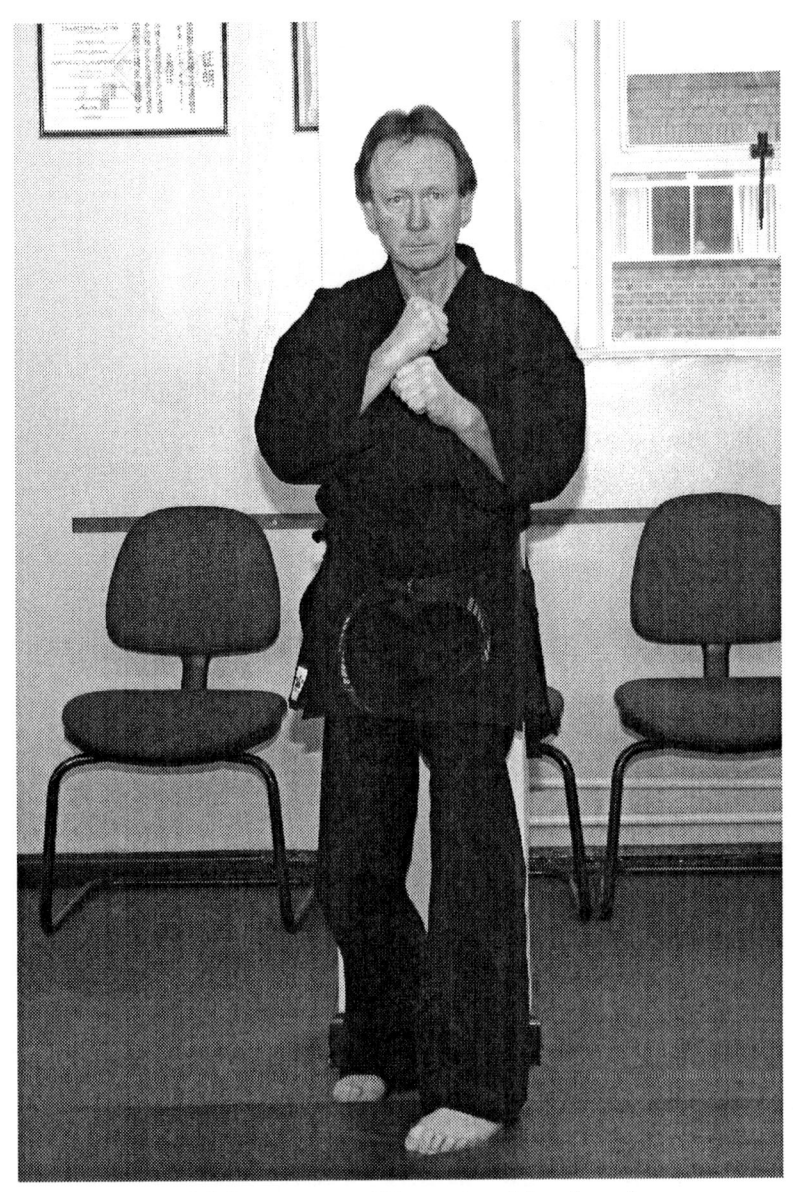

Wall fighting stance Illustration 64, a, b and c.

James Moclair

Illustration 64, b and c,

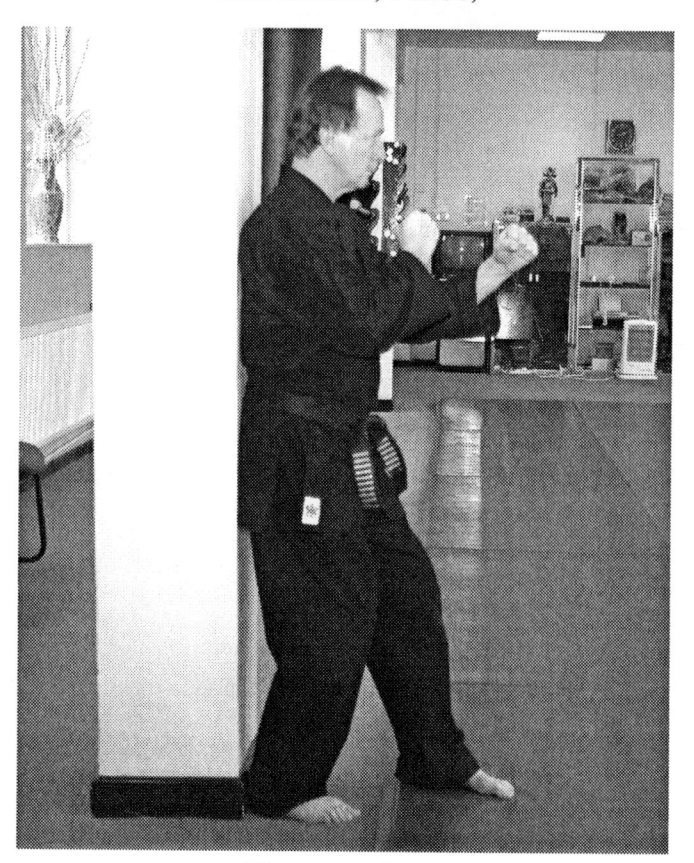

Illustration 64, c.

A Breath Of Fresh Air

Defence Against A Wall

In the "Wall Posture Position" this position the head should be more or less impossible to be push back into the wall. You can practice this with a partner by you standing back to a wall and adopting the wall posture position. Get your partner to grab a hold of your lapel with his/her left hand and with the right hand place it under your chin and then try to push your head towards the wall. (When practising this keep your tongue away from your teeth.)

This position is also the attack that I will explain how to defend from.

The attacker has pushed me against the wall by grabbing my lapel with his left hand, and driving me backward by pushing with the right hand under my chin. I have immediately come into the wall stance position as shown in illustration 65, a, and 1b.

Illustration 65, a

Attacker ties to drive my head into the wall
Illustration 65 1 b

James Moclair

Place the right hand on the attackers left shoulder, with the left hand grab hold of the attacker's right forearm as shown in illustration 65, b. The left hand should be placed on top of the attacker's right arm.

Illustration 65, b   Elbow strike the attacker Illustration 65, c.

Step sharply to the left side with both feet and with the right hand pull the attacker forward at the same time pull outward with the left hand this will result in the attacker falling forward into the wall. Now strike with the right elbow to the nape of the attacker's neck. This will drive the attackers head into the wall as shown in illustration 65, c.

A Breath Of Fresh Air

Pull the attacker's right arm out straight. With the right arm reach over the attacker's right arm and grab a hold of your left arm. Put pressure on the attacker elbow by pulling down with the right arm and lifting up left hand. This will apply an elbow lock and also keep him trapped against the wall. As shown in illustration 65, d and 65, d a..

Applying an elbow lock Illustration 65, d.

Illustration 65, d, a. Elbow locking the attacker's right arm

To finalize this routine, heel kick the back of the attacker's knee as shown in illustration 65, e. Kiai with the heel kick.

Illustration 65, e.

Return to fighting stance as son as you complete the kick.

A Breath Of Fresh Air

Floor Fighting Stance

The next illustration shows me on the floor/mats in floor fighting stance. This is the stance that should be adopted if you are in the predicament of having to defend yourself from the floor. I know what your thinking, I am learning martial arts to defend myself and anyone worth there salt won't be stupid enough to get down on the floor when being attacked. Well in the real world an extremely high percentage of fights ends up with a tussle and roll around on the floor. We are all human, it is easy to loose your footing or balance and end up on your back. So we have train for all eventualities. Now lets get back to the floor fighting stance lie on your back head up of the floor hands up in the guard position, have your hands to the side the potential attack is coming from Drop your chin down and bend both knees up, pointing the knees upward so this take the groin area of line as shown in illustration 66,a.

Floor fighting stance. Illustration 66, a.

Floor Defence Against A Kick To The Head

The attacker has approached from my left side, he has is left leg forward. I immediately adopt the floor fighting stance as shown in illustration 67, a. I hope you like the attacker's socks. We thought it might help with the photos. Ok I'll come clean his feet were cold.

Illustration 67,a.

Next the attacker swings a kick to my head, using his right foot. I have moved in and blocked the foot with my left arm, with a reverse outside forearm block. Time the block so you stop the kick just as his foot is about to leave the floor. As shown in illustration 67, b.

Attacker swings a kick to the head. Illustration 67, b.

As soon as the block is completed, take a hold of the of the attackers ankle with the right hand as shown in illustration 67,c.

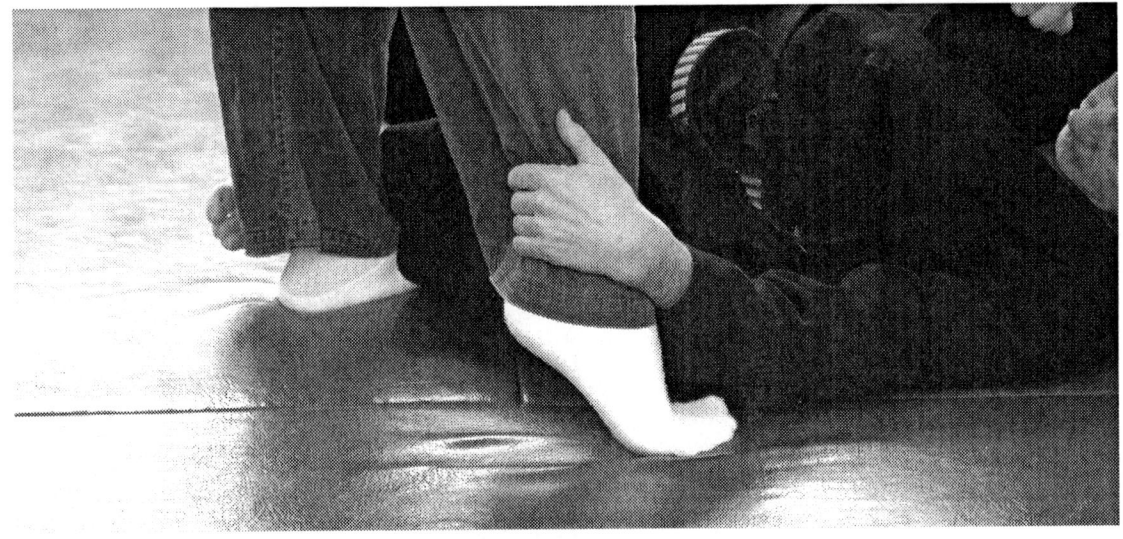

Illustration 67, c.

The socks really do work, I think it might start a fashion in the martial arts fraternity.

In a nice smooth movement, move in close to the attacker and with the right leg, bend from the knee and hook the right foot around the attackers left ankle joint as shown in illustration 67, d.

Illustration 67, d.

The right hand shoots out and is placed on the attacker's right knee. This will now start to break the attacker's balance, as shown in illustration 67, e.

Illustration 67, e.

A Breath Of Fresh Air

With the right leg, side kick the attackers stomach at the same time pull with left hand and push with the right hand, this will completely unbalance him and throw to the floor. As shown in illustration 67, f and 67, g. don't be tempted to kick the attacker in the groin, kicking him in the groin will result in him collapsing on top you.

Side kick the attacker Illustration 67, f.

Attacker hit the floor after being kicked. Illustration 67, g.

Finally, execute a floor axe kick to the attacker's groin. To do this place both hands on the floor, the hands are about shoulders width apart. Bend the left knee up and lift your body of the floor. As you are doing this raise the right leg as high as you can and then drop it in an axe like motion using the heel of the foot to strike the attackers groin. As shown in illustration 67, h. Kiai with the floor axe kick.

Illustration 67, h.

As soon as you have completed the floor axe kick get yourself up into a standing fighting stance.

Floor Defence With The Attacker Doing A Kick To The Ribs

For the next defence routine the attacker has come in on my left side with his left leg forward. I have immediately adopted the floor fighting stance, as shown in illustration 68, a.

Illustration 68, a.

The attacker throws a kick with his right foot, to the rib area. As soon as his foot leaves the floor, block the kick with your left arm, with a downward sweeping block. Your forearm should make contact with the top of the attacker foot by his ankle joint as shown in illustration 68, b.

The attacker throws a kick to the rib cage Illustration 68, b.

James Moclair

Leave the blocking arm on top of the attacker foot and bend from left knee and move your left leg right behind the attacker's right leg so that you trap his foot as shown in illustration 68, c.

Trapping the attacker's right foot. Illustration 68, c.

Shoot the right hand out and place your hand on the attackers left knee, pushing with the right hand will start to break the attackers balance. As shown in illustration 68, d.

Illustration 68, d.

Do a side kick to the attacker's stomach with your right foot, using the heel to strike. At the same time keep pushing with the right hand. Both actions will throw the attacker to the floor. As shown in illustration 68, d and 68, e. Remember do not kick the attacker in the groin, he will only collapse on you and cause you further suffering.

Attacker is thrown to the floor. Illustration 68, e

Lift yourself up so that both the right and left palms are flat on the floor and your arms are straight. Balance on the left foot and kick the attacker using the ball of your foot with the right foot in his solar plexus. As shown in illustration 68, f. Kiai with the kick

Illustration 68, f.

As son as you have completed the kick return to a standing fighting stance.

Defence From Strangle On The Floor

In the next attack, the attacker has managed to force me to the floor and is trying to strangle me. He is on both knees and to my right side. To help protect my head I have raised my head of the floor, this also help reduce the amount of neck area the attacker can grip. Further I have bent both of my knees up so that I have some posture, as shown in illustration 69, a.

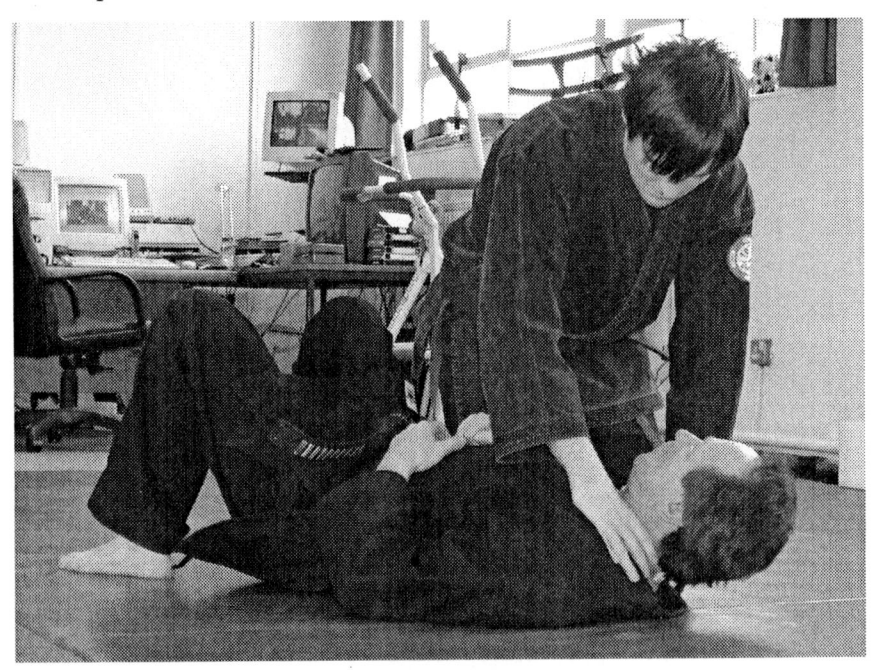

Illustration 69, a.

Reach up with the right hand and place it on the attacker's right shoulder. With the left hand reach up and place under the attacker's right armpit and turn your body as far as you can towards the attacker, as shown in illustration 69, b.

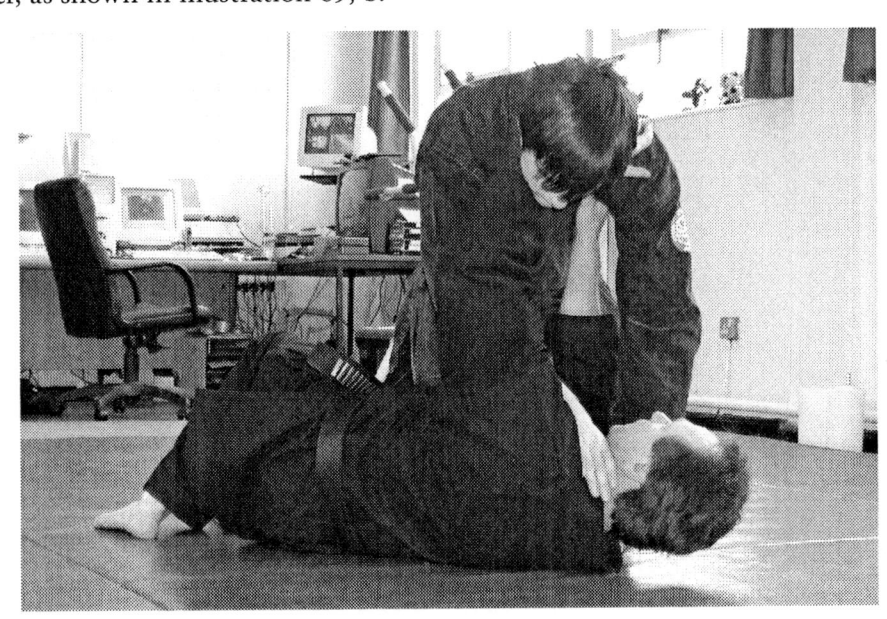

Illustration 69, b.

Turn sharply with your body from right to left, pulling with the right hand and at the same time push with the left to throw the attacker across your body. As shown in illustration 69, c.

Illustration 69, c.

Continue the pull and push action until the attacker has been thrown completely from your right side to your left side. With the right hand still on the attacker right shoulder, pull the shoulder toward you and bear with your forearm against the attackers wind pipe to apply a strangulation technique, as shown in illustration 69, d.

Illustration 69, d.

A Breath Of Fresh Air

With the left hand, place it on the attackers left elbow and draw the attackers left arm towards your right shoulder and at the same time let go of the attackers left shoulder with the right hand. Now place the right hand on the attackers left elbow and apply pressure by pulling down. This will apply an elbow crush. As shown in illustration 69, e and close up of elbow crush in illustration 69, e, a .

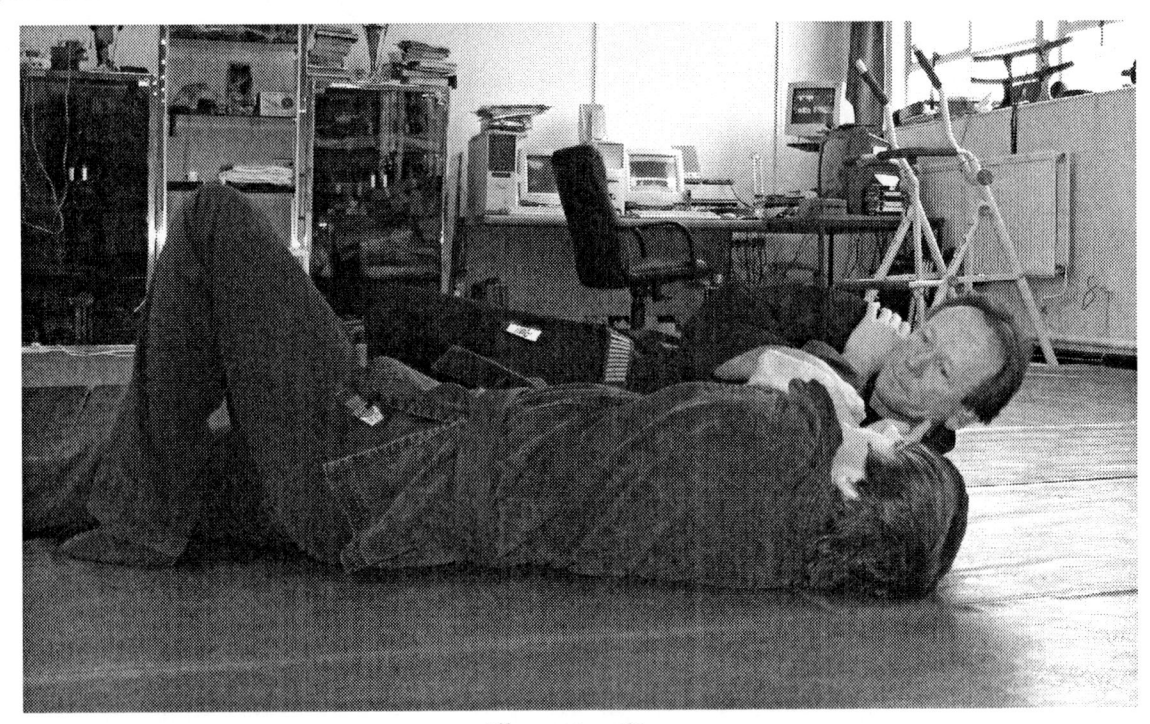

Illustration 69, e.

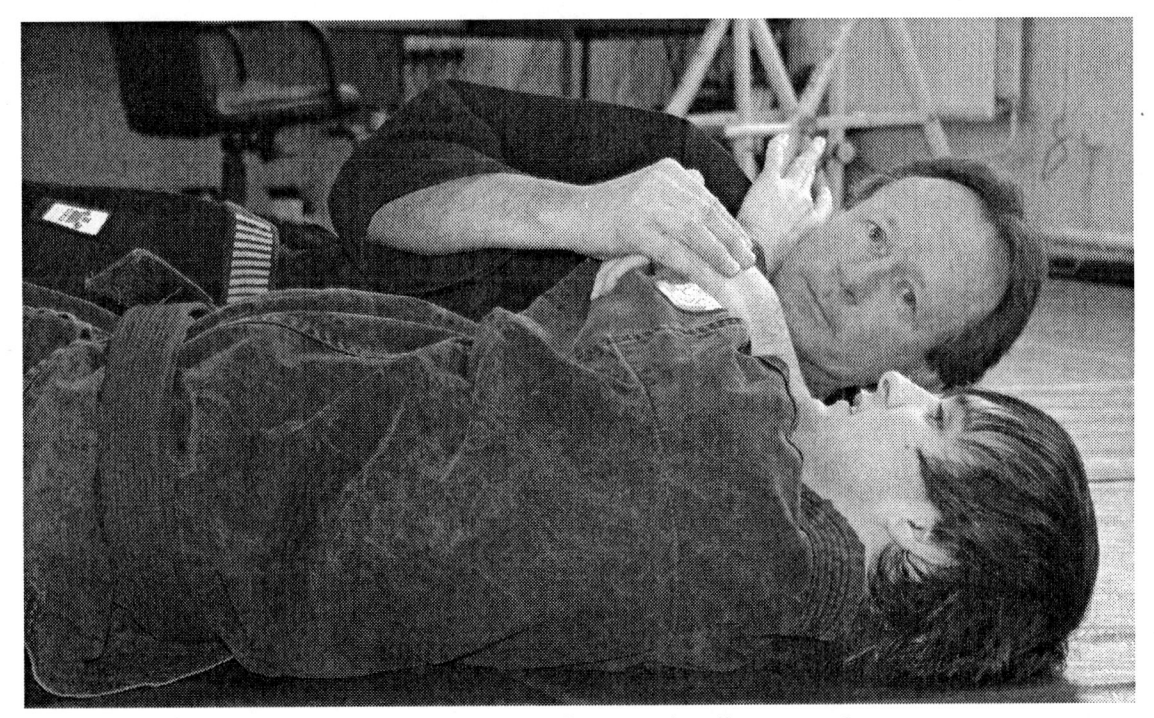

Close up of hands applying elbow crush.   Illustration 69, e, a.

175

To finalize this routine keep the elbow crush on the attacker and with the right foot, heel kick the attacker in the groin as shown in illustration 69, f.

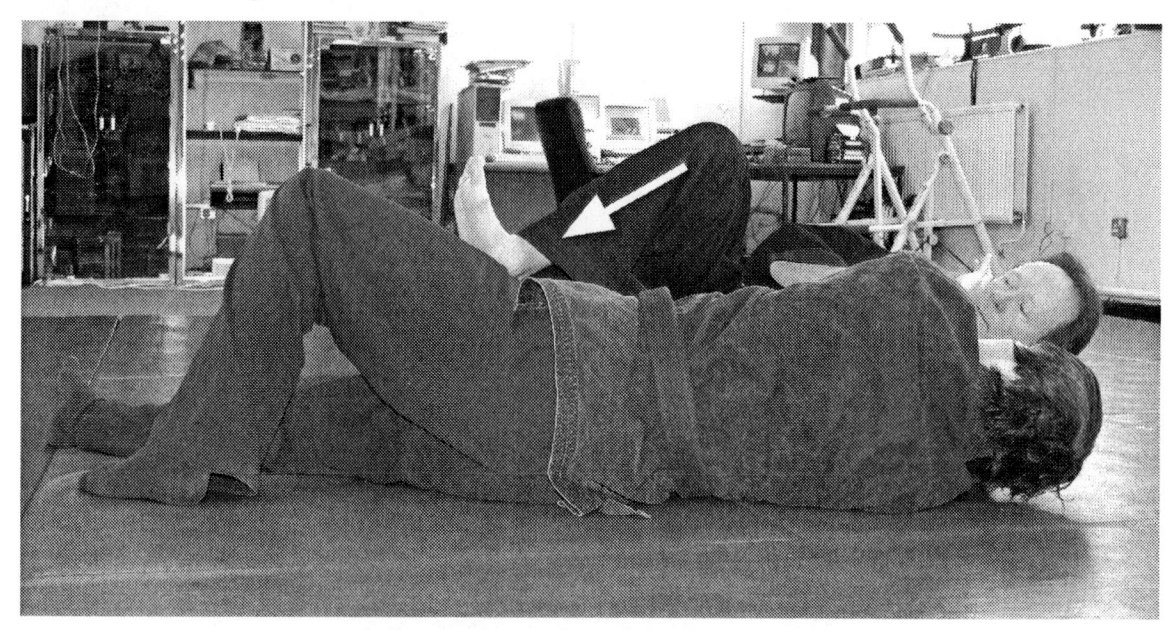

Kick the attacker in the groin. Illustration 69, f.

As soon as you have completed the heel kick to the groin, disengage the elbow lock and get yourself up to a standing fighting stance.

A Breath Of Fresh Air

Front Kick Defence

The attacker has squared up to me in fighting stance with his left leg forward. I have applied the distance rule and come into fighting stance with my left leg forward. As shown in illustration 70, a.

Illustration 70, a

The attacker then tries to do a front kick to your body with his right leg. To avoid the front kick, you will need to have preformed a quarter step by moving the left foot to your left side and at the same time move the right foot to your left side. I have explain the quarter step procedure earlier in this book so if you are not to sure how to do this refer to illustrations 27,a. As you perform the quarter step use the right arm to help parry the kick away from you by timing this so as the kick comes towards you scoop your right arm under the attacker's right leg as shown in illustration 70, b.

Illustration 70, b.

Drop your right arm down and in a smooth arc retreat your right and then left feet so that you are positioned at the rear of the attacker. Please take note of the arrow on the illustration 70,c to help with the leg movements. Place both hands on the attacker's shoulders as shown in illustration 70 c.

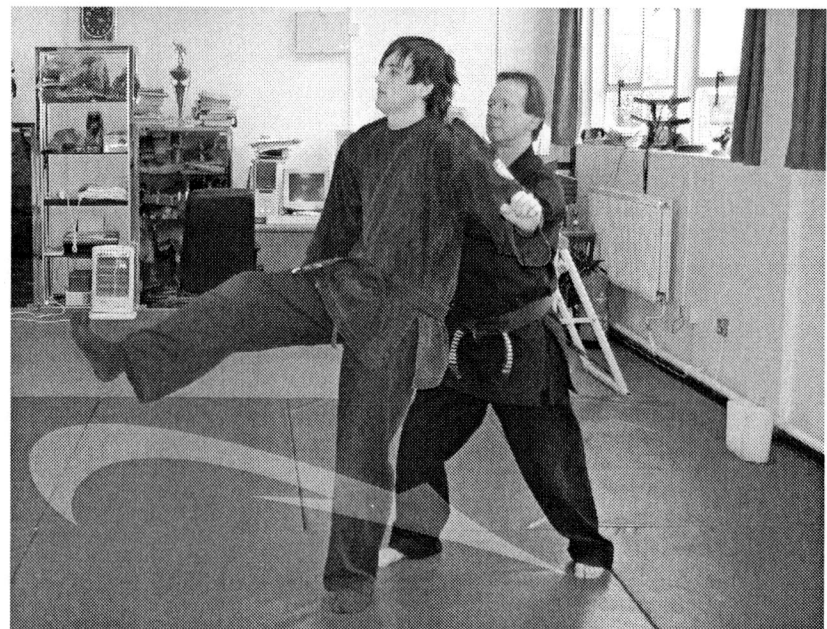

Illustration 70, c.

If this technique was employed out in the street, you can take a hold of anything that is available to you, for example, if the person kicking at you has a pony tail, you could grab this instead of the shoulders. Long hair, ears with ear rings and jackets with hood also work well also.

Continue reversing the right foot a little further and pull on the attacker's shoulders to get him of balance. As shown in illustration 70, d.

Illustration 70, d.

With a good pull on the attackers shoulders, throw him to the floor as shown in illustration 70, e.

Illustration 70, e.

From evading the kick, the leg work should be done in one smooth movement and is completed when the attacker hits the floor. Like everything this takes practice, so once you have done this a few hundred thousand times on both sides you will be able to do this technique without thinking about it, and that is what martial arts is all about.

To complete the routine raise the right leg up and do a heel kick to the attackers solar plexus. As shown in illustration 70, f and 70, g.

Illustration 70, f.

Heel kick, the attacker. Illustration 70, g.

Kiai with the heel kick and then return back to fighting stance.

Side Kick Defence

The attacker has approached me in a fighting stance and has his left leg forward. I have immediately come into fighting stance, with my left leg forward and have applied the distance rule. As shown in illustration 71, a.

Illustration 71, a.

The attacker fires a right side kick to the chest area. To avoid the kick quarter step to your left side, at the same time scoop your right arm under the attacker,s kicking leg catching his leg by his ankle joint. The ideal point to on your right arm to catch the side kick is where your arm bends at the elbow joint. As shown in illustration 71, b.

Illustration 71,b.

Now with the left hand place it on the attacker's right knee. As shown in illustration 71, c.

Illustration 71, c

As soon as your left hand is in place, kneel down onto your left knee, this will start to break the attackers balance as shown in illustration 71, d.

Illustration 71, d.

With right and left hand pull the attacker from your right to your left to throw the attacker to the floor as shown in illustration 71, d.

Throw the attacker to the floor. Illustration 71, d.

Have your left hand palm down and have it positioned just above the attacker knee cap. Place your right arm under the attacker right leg and have your right hand on top of left and grip the

James Moclair

left hand with the right. Pull both hand towards you to lock the attackers knee joint at the same time scoop upward to dislocate the attackers knee cap

The angle of the attacker leg is very important, have the leg at about 45 degrees. As shown in illustration 71, e and also the close shoot of the hand positions in 71, f.

Illustration 71, e

Care should be taken when practising this knee lock and knee cap dislocation, as it is very easy to pop the knee cap.

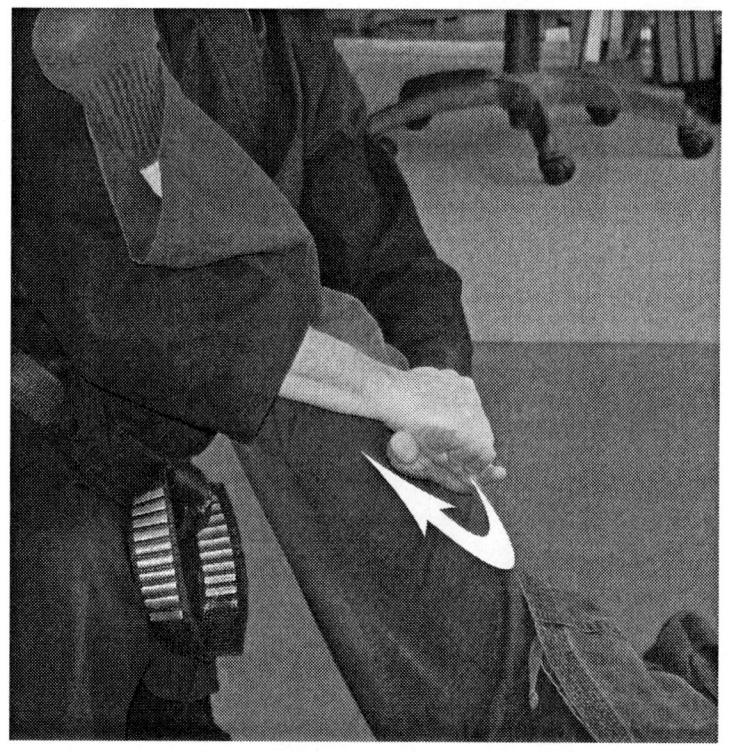

Illustration 71, f.

Push the attacker's right leg down to the floor with your left hand and draw the right hand back ready to punch him in the groin. As shown in illustration 71, h.

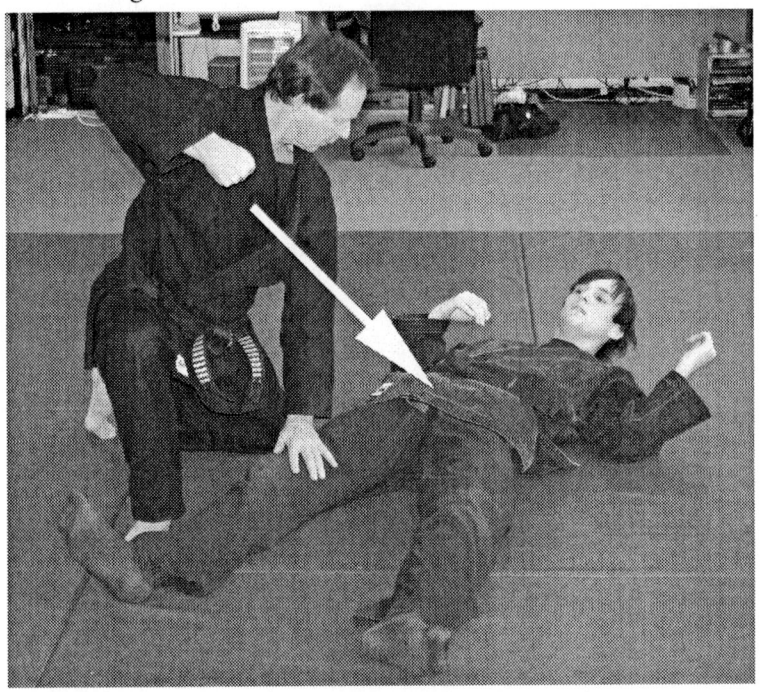

Illustration 71, h.

To finalize this routine, strike the attacker in the groin with the right fist, as shown in illustration 71, i. Kiai with the punch.

Punch the attacker in the groin. Illustration 71, I.

As soon as you finish the punch to the groin return to fighting stance.

James Moclair

Round House Kick Defence

The attacker has approached me and has come into fighting stance with his left leg forward. I have also adopted the fighting stance with my left leg forward and applied the distance rule as shown in illustration 72, a.

Illustration 72, a.

The attacker throws a roundhouse kick to the rib area. To defend yourself from this kick you will need to blend in the rotational force of the kick, that is to say, turn your body in the direction the kick is coming. From the fighting stance with the left leg forward reverse the left leg in an arc as indicated by the arrow on illustration 72, b. As you are reversing the left leg back try to tuck your body as close as you can into the attackers upper thigh. At the same time bring the left arm under the attacker's right leg and have the right arm over the attacker's right leg, and take a hold with both hands. As shown in illustration 72, b.

Illustration 72, b.

Continue to reverse back with the left leg and now place your right foot at the back of the attackers left foot; this will set the attacker up for a throw to the floor. As shown in illustration 72, c.

Illustration 72, c.

With both hands pull the attacker right leg from your right side to you're to your left side this will throw the attacker to the floor as shown in illustration 72, d.

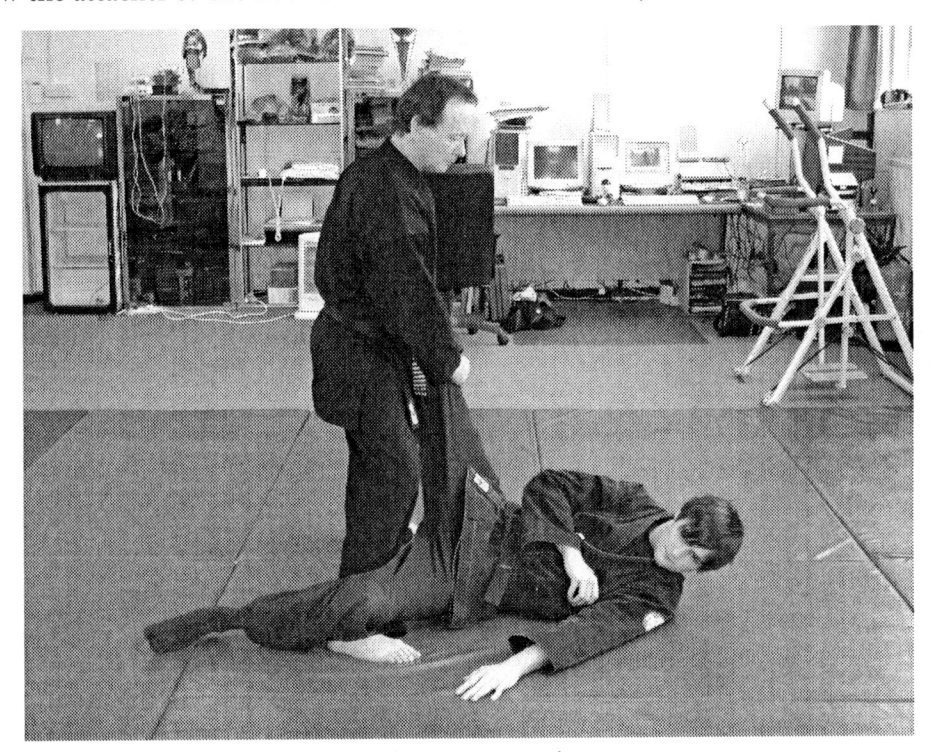

Illustration 72, d.

Now with the left hand grab hold of the attacker's right leg and push his leg away to your left side. At the same time trap the attackers left leg with your right knee and push outward so the attacker legs are stretched as far as they will go. As shown in illustration 72, e.

Illustration 72, e

If the attacker is not very supple this action will cause him considerable discomfort, it also stops him trying to kick out at you from the floor.

To finalize the routine keep the pressure on by still pushing with the left hand and stretching the attacker out with the right knee. As your right hand is free and the attacker is in an extremely prone position, punch him in the groin and remember to kiai. As shown in illustration 72, f.

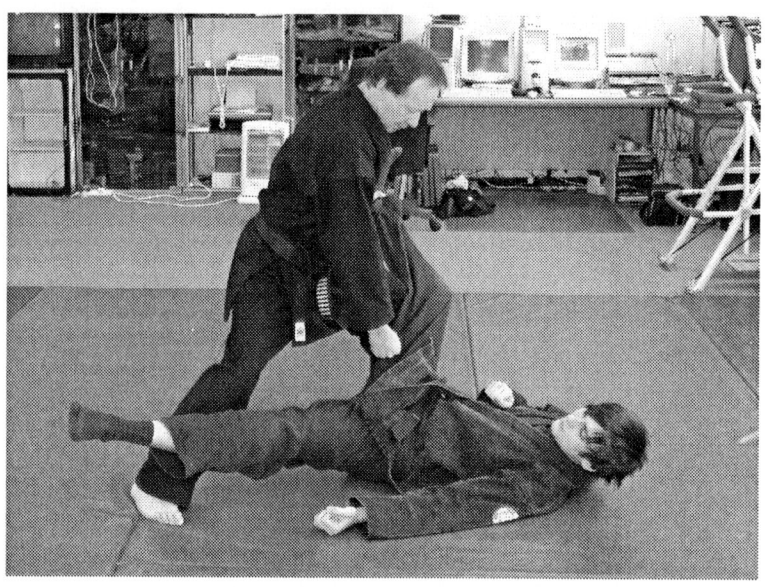

Illustration 72, f

Return to a fighting stance as soon as you have completed the strike to the groin.

Turning Back Kick

For this routine the attacker has taken a fighting stance with his left leg forward. I have also taken a fighting stance with my left leg forward; I have also applied the distance rule. As shown in illustration 73 a.

Illustration 73, a.

The attacker steps with his left leg to his right so that his back is to me as he starts the turn of the turning back kick. As shown in illustration 73,b.

Illustration 73, b.

The step across by the attacker can be a faint to lull you into thinking that he may be retreating from the attack so be on your guard.

The attacker throws a kick backward towards me. To avoid the turning back kick from fighting stance with the left leg forward quarter step to the left and immediately advance forward with the left leg. Place the left hand on the attackers right shoulder and start to push forward, this will start to unbalance the attacker. At the same time, strike the attacker in the groin with the right hand using the ridge hand strike as shown in illustration 73, c.

Illustration73, c.

Continue to push forward with the left hand so that the attacker falls forward. Have the right hand under the attacker's right leg as you will need to keep control of his leg to finalize the routine. Illustration 73 d shows the attacker falling forward and the position of the hands.

Illustration 73, d.

As the attacker continues to fall forward, let both of your hands slide along his right leg and grasp his ankle joint. Keep the attackers leg up to about your waist height as shown in illustration 73, e.

Illustration 73, e.

To conclude this routine keep the attacker's right leg raised up, this puts him in a nice position for a painful kick in the groin. Now with your right foot give the good news. Illustration 73, f shows the attacker receiving the good news. Kiai, with the kick.

Kick the attacker in the groin. Illustration 73, f.

Return to fighting stance on completion of the "good news kick".

Forearm Nelson Attack

For the next defence routine, the attack will be done from a forearm nelson. I realise that not everyone knows what a forearm nelson is so I have put a couple of illustrations in so that you can see what the attack looks like and a written explanation.

How To Do A Forearm Nelson

The attacker comes from the rear and gets both hands under your both arms. He then continues to reach up and clasps his hand at the back of your neck. He applies pressure by pushing down. I have to say this is a particularly dangerous attack that could break your neck and leave you paralyzed so you definitely need to know how to defend yourself from this neck lock. Illustrations 74, a. and 74, b. show the forearm nelson at different angles.

Forearm nelson attack. Illustration 74, a   Illustration 74, b.

Forearm nelson, note the where the attackers hand is.

A Breath Of Fresh Air

Now let's start with the defence from the forearm nelson attack. Come into posture straight away by stepping forward with the left leg. As the attacker puts his arms under your arms trap both his arms by extending your arms forward about 15 degrees and push inward as hard as you can. This will result in foiling the attacker attempts at getting his up to the back of your neck. It will also trap the attacker's arms and he will not be able to withdraw them. As shown in illustration 75, a.

Attacker tries to put a forearm nelson hold on.
Illustration 75, a

Illustration 75, b

With your right hand take a hold of the attacker's right hand as shown in illustration 75, b.

James Moclair

Keep a hold of the attacker's right hand and turn to your right side and elbow strike the attacker in the side of his face. As you start your turn release the attackers left arm. As shown in illustrations 75,c. and 75, d.

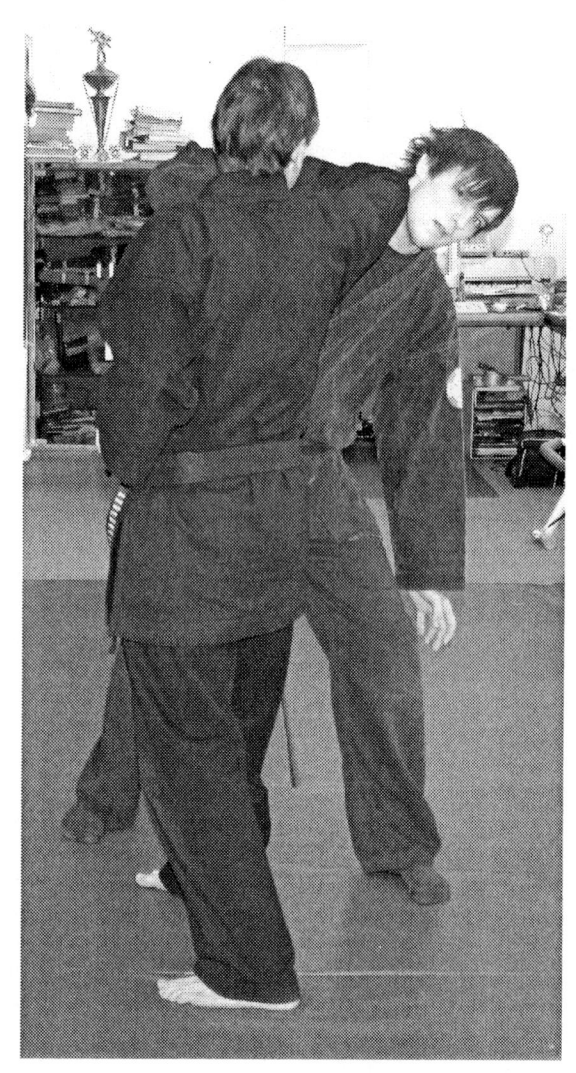

Illustration 75, c

Illustration 75, d. Shows a different camera angle of the elbow strike

The elbow strike will also set the attacker up for a wrist lock, as you turn to complete the elbow strike make sure that the attackers right arm is bent at the elbow joint. This should happen automatically by virtue of your body position in relation to the attacker's body position.

Keep a hold with the right hand and with your left hand take a hold of the attacker's right hand. The attacker should start to feel pressure and a little pain in his wrist joint. As shown in illustration 75, e.

Illustration 75, e.

Step back with your right leg and start to push down to make the wrist lock more powerful. As shown in illustration 75, f.

Left side view. Illustration 75, f.

James Moclair

The position of your hands and fingers are very important, your right hand should be holding at the back of the attacker's right hand. Your fingers are gripping the outer edges of his hand and your thumb should be placed between the attackers thumb and first finger. Your left hand takes hold of the attacker's right at the hand and wrist. As shown in illustration 75, g.

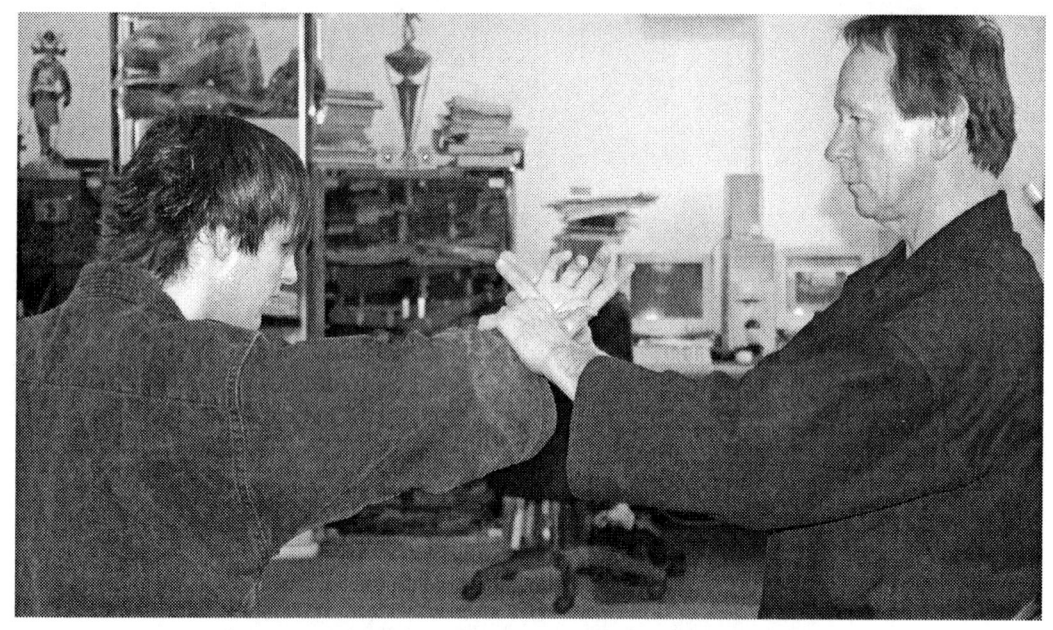

Close up of the left hand and wrist lock. Illustration 75, g.

To assist with this wrist lock, the following illustrations are taken out a different angle, so that you can see both sides of the wrist lock and where the right hand is placed. Illustration 75, h shows the left side of the wrist lock.

Left side of the wrist lock. Illustration 75, h.

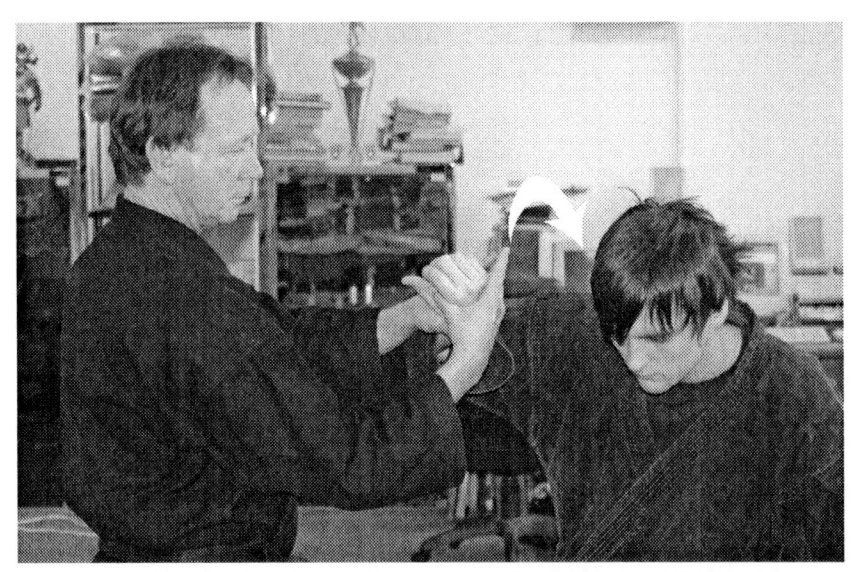

Illustration 75, i shows the correct position of the right hand.

I always point my index fingers and only grip with my other fingers and thumbs. The pointing of the index finger is for the flow of Ki (Internal power). Try pointing your index finger and see if it improves the wrist lock technique. With the hands in the correct position apply downward pressure to the attacker's wrist and at the same time try pointing the index finger to the attacker's stomach, at the same time breath out sharply.

A quick word of warning do, not bang this wrist lock on to your training partner or you will break his or her wrist.

As soon as you apply pressure to the wrist the attacker under pain will drop to his knees. As shown in illustration 75, j.

Illustration 75, j

James Moclair

To finish the routine, keep the wrist lock on the attacker and kick him in the groin using the top of your foot as shown in illustration 75, k. Kiai with the kick.

Illustration 75, k.

Return to a fighting stance once you have completed the groin kick.

Side Head Lock

So that the reader understands what a side head lock is, the following illustration shows the attacker gripping my head with his right and left arms and pulling me forward so that my posture is completely broken. As shown in illustration 76, a.

The attacker has me in a side head lock. Illustration 76, a.

If you are caught in a side head lock it can be a powerful hold and extremely painful especially if the attacker has good upper body strength. So now let's look at how the stop this hold being applied.

As soon as the attacker puts his right arm around your neck, you must block him from pulling you forward by pushing your left sided hip into his right buttock. Brace your body so that you cannot be pulled forward. At the same time use your right arm to block the attackers left arm so that he cannot reach up and take a hold of his right hand. As shown in illustration 76, b.

Block the attacker using your right hip. Illustration 76, b.

The bock with the right hand should be done with the hand open so that you can take an immediate hold of the attackers left arm.

With your left hand, reach over the attacker's right shoulder and put your hand on his chin and pull backwards. At the same time, take a hold of the attackers left arm with your right hand so that he cannot strike out at you as shown in illustration 76, c.

Illustration 76, c.

Stepping back with your left leg and pulling back with the hand on the attackers chin will draw the attacker off balance. At the same time let go of the attacker left arm and raise your right arm up, have your hand open and ready to strike with a flexible palm heel strike. As shown in illustration 76, d.

Illustration 76, d.

Use the flexible palm heel, to strike to the attackers solar plexus, as you do this remember to kiai.

While still pulling back with the right hand, strike with the left hand and palm heel to the attacker's solar plexus and follow through so that it knocks the attacker to the floor as shown in illustration 76, e.

Follow through with the palm heel strike. Illustration 76, e.

James Moclair

To finish of this routine raise the left leg up and heel kick the attacker in the lower abdomen. As shown in illustration 76, f. Kiai with the heel kick.

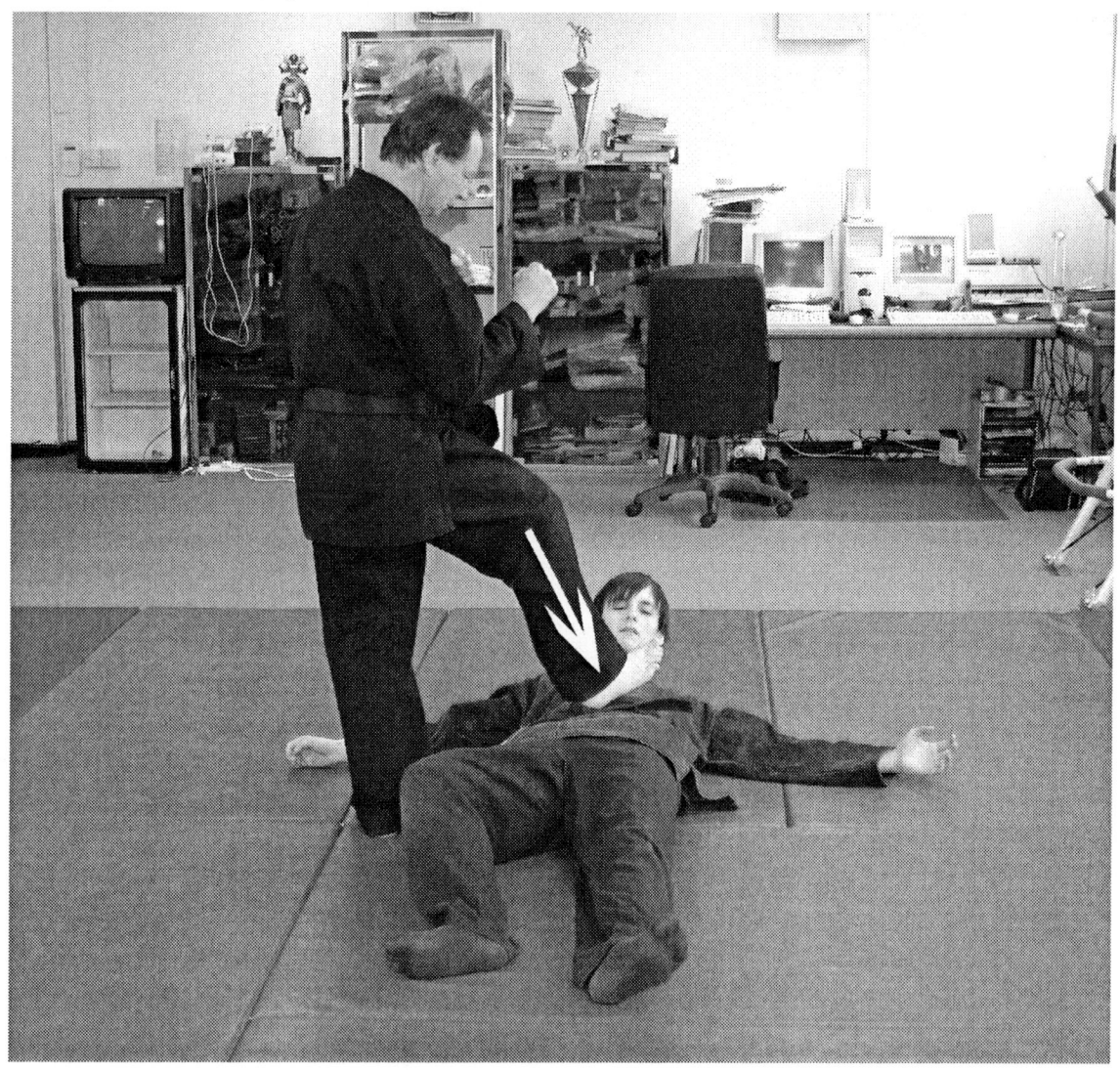

Heel kick the attacker. Illustration 76, f.

Return to fighting stance as soon as you do the heel kick.

The heel kick to the lower abdomen has some interesting side effects, not only will it cause the attacker severe stomach pain….. What if prior to him attacking you he has just downed sixteen pints of lager followed by a large Indian curry, this might cause a mouth gusher…… So get yourself away quickly.

Another interesting thought is what if he has had a couple of bad pints and the curry was off. This could result in the famous Deli Belly……I will let you ponder on that one.

Back Leg Crescent Kick

For this kick take a partner and equip your partner with an appropriate focus pad. The black pad I use in the following illustrations is ideal for the crescent kicks. Stand in fighting stance with the left leg forward as shown in illustration 77,a

Illustration 77, a.

With your right leg swing it in an arc like motion aiming it towards to focus pad. Keep both your arms up to help with your balance as shown in illustration 77, b

Illustration 77, b.

Strike the focus pad with the sole of your foot. You can achieve this by angling the ankle joint so that the sole of your foot is pointing to the focus pad as shown in illustration 77, c.

Hit the focus pad with the sole of your foot. Illustration 77, c.

Continue the crescent kick through, so that your right foot lands on the floor to the right side of the attacker. The arrow in illustration 77, d indicates the decent of your leg after striking the focus pad.

Illustration 77, d.

Once your foot lands on the floor, you have completed the kick so now you can return back to fighting stance. Remember to kiai with the kick.

When doing a crescent kick always follow through with the kick. You should never do a crescent kick and then immediately after pull your leg back after hitting the target, this will only result in a groin strain or muscle injury to the inner thigh.

Front Leg Crescent Kick

Stand in fighting stance with the right foot forward as shown in illustration 78, a.

Illustration 78, a.

Bring you left foot to your right foot and bend slightly from the knees as shown in illustration 78, b.

Illustration 78, b.

The bending of the knees helps give you upward lift, and upward lift is vital for power in the kick and also for height.

James Moclair

As with the back leg crescent kick, swing the right leg in an arc and strike the focus pad with the sole of your foot as shown in illustration 78, c.

Strike the focus pad with the sole of your foot. Illustration 78, c.

Follow the crescent kick through and end up in fighting stance as shown in illustration 78, d.

Illustration 78, d.

Jumping Crescent Kick

To put a jump in with the kick allows you to make up a greater distance between you and the attacker. You can also achieve greater height by jumping with the kick.

The kick should be done in one flowing motion; however this will require lots of practice, so let's get cracking.

Stand with your right leg forward in fighting stance, as shown in illustration 79, a.

Illustration 79, a.

James Moclair

Raise the left leg up as high as you can and point it at the attackers left shoulder. At the same time bend slightly from the left knee, this will help with balance and also help with the upward lift in the jump. As shown in illustration 79, b.

Illustration 79, b.

Now with the right leg, jump up in the air and throw the right leg in a arc towards the focus pad. The right leg should pass over the left leg and then the left leg descends back to the floor a shown in illustration 79, c.

Illustration 79, c.

Strike the focus pad with the sole of your foot. To help with counter balance drop the right hand down and keep the left hand up as shown in illustration 79, d.

Illustration 79, d.

The white arrow in the illustration above shows the direction of the right leg after striking the focus pad and where the right foot will land.

Follow the kick through and land in a fighting stance as shown in illustration 79, d.

Reverse Jumping Crescent Kick

Attacks can come in at every conceivable angle, so you need to be able to kick in all directions. The reverse jumping crescent kick deals with the attacker approaching you from the rear.

To practice this kick stand in fighting stance, have the right leg forward with your back to your partner as shown in illustration 80, a.

Illustration 80, a.

Bending from the left knee, raise the left leg up as high as you can. At the same time; standing on one foot, turn to face the attacker. Stop when your knee is pointing to the attackers left shoulder. As you turn, keep a small bend in the right knee to help with upward lift. The arrow in illustration s 80, b shows the rotation of your knee.

Illustration 80, b.

Now, with the right leg jump into the air and thrust your right foot in an arc to hit the focus pad. As you hit the focus pad drop the left leg down so that you are now standing on the left foot. As shown in illustration 80, c.

Illustration 80, c.

Continue through with the kick and finish in a fighting stance, right leg forward. As shown in illustration 80, d.

Illustration 80, d.

Back Leg Reverse Crescent Kick

Stand in fighting stance with the left leg forward as shown in illustration 81, a.

Illustration 81, a.

Move the right foot from the closed position to the open position by pivoting on left heel as shown in illustration 81, b.

Illustration 81, b.

A Breath Of Fresh Air

With the right leg swing it in a circular motion and strike the focus pad with the outer edge of your foot. Avoid making contact with the ankle joint as this will result in injury. Illustration 81, c shows the circular motion with an arrow pointing in the direction your foot should travel.

Illustration 81, c.

Once you foot hits the focus pad, continue the kick on through. Never pull back on the kick as this will result in groin or inner thigh injury. Illustration 81, d shows the correct foot direction after you have hit the focus pad.

Illustration 81, d.

James Moclair

As you put your right foot back on the floor, it should bring you back into fighting stance with the left leg forward. As shown in illustration 81, e.

Illustration 81, e.

Front Leg Reverse Crescent Kick

Stand in fighting stance with the right leg forward as shown in illustration 82, a.

Illustration 82, a.

With the left leg, step so that both your feet are together. At the same time bend from both knees to help with uplift. As shown in illustration 82, b.

Illustration 82, b.

With the right foot swing it in a circular motion and strike the focus pad with the outer edge of your foot. The arrow in illustration 82, c shows you the direction the right foot takes from the floor and towards the focus pad

Illustration 82, c.

Continue the kick through and land your right foot on the floor and come immediately into fighting stance. The white arrow in illustration 82, d show the angle of the right foot as it strikes the focus pad and then the route that it follows to the floor.

Illustration 82, d.

With the crescent kicks done, that also completes the yellow to orange belt syllabus for kempo karate. I think you will agree that from the novice to the orange belt it is a comprehensive syllabus and one that has a lot of practical techniques and defences.

However the journey has only just started, where it ends is up to you. The foundation has now been laid and the scope to build a fantastic martial artist is now on the horizon. I hope I will see you there.

Best Wishes, Soyonara

James Moclair

Japanese Terminology And Glossary - A through Z

A

Abara: The ribs
Age: Rising
Age: Uke: Rising block
Ago: Jaw
Ago Uchi: A Strike to the Jaw
Ai Hanmi: Aikido Posture where both Exponents have the same Foot Forward
Aiki: Union of Energy. Harmony with Energy.
Aikido: A way of Harmony with **Ki**. Founed in 1920 by **Ueshiba Morihei**
Aikijutsu: Older Art of Aikido, Style Descended from the **Daito Ryu.**
Ashi: Leg, Foot
Ashi Garami: Leg Entanglement Technique
Ashi Guruma: Leg Wheel
Ashi waza: Foot techniques
Atemi: A Strike to a Weak or Vital Point on the Body
Atemi Waza: Striking Techniques Used to Weak or Vital Points on the Body

B

Bajutsu: The art of Horse Riding
Batto: To Draw and Cut with a Blade
Bo: Wood Staff around 5' to 6' long
Bo-jutsu: The Art of using a **Bo**
Bogyo: Defence
Bokken: Wooden Sword, one that resembles a **Katana**
Boshi; Thumb
Bo Tanto: Wooden Training Knife
Bo Naginata: Wooden Polearm
Budo: Martial way
Budoka: A Person Studying Martial Arts
Bugei: Martial Art; the name for Comprehensive Classical Japanese Combative Systems
Bugeisha: A Practitioner of **Bugie**
Bujin: Warrior Person; Low Ranking **Samurai**
Bu-Jutsu: Catch All Term for all Japanese Martial Arts
Buki: Weapons
Buki-ho: Methods of using Weapons
Bunkai: Analysis of **Kata.** The True MeaningBehind the moves in **Karate Kata**
Bushi: Another word for **Samurai**
Bushido: The Way of the **Samurai**

C

Chi: Earth

Chiburi: Ritualized Shaking of Sword to Remove Blood
Choku tsuke: Straight Punch
Chuden: Mid Level
Chuden choku tsuki: Straight Punch to Middle of Body

D

Dachi: Stance
Daicho: Large Intestine
Dai: Large, Big
Dai Kinniku: Major Muscles
Dai Nippon Butokukai: An Martial Arts Organization First Established in 1895 in **Kyoto** Japan
Daisho: Pair Of Swords worn by the **Samurai**. A Long and a Short Sword.
Daitai: The thigh (also **momo**)
Dan: Rank; Denotes Black Belt Ranks. Ranks increase from 1 – 10.
De Ashi Harai: Advancing Foot Sweep.
Dembu: Buttocks
Denko: Atemi Point at the Floating Ribs.
Deshi: Student
Do: The Way.
Dojo: Place for Practicing an Art or Skill.
Dokko: Pressure Point behind the Ear.

E

Empi: Elbow
Empi Uchi: Elbow Strike
Empi Waza: Elbow Techniques.
Empi Uke: Elbow Block
Enga Osae: To pin face down
En Sho: Round Heel
Eri: Collar or Lapel.
Eri Dori: Lapel Grab
Eri Jime: A Strangulation Technique Using the Lapels
Eri Seoinage: A Judo Throw Done by Grabbing the Opponents Lapels

F

Fudo Dachi: Rooted Stance
Fuku Shidoin: Assistant Instructor
Fukushiki Kokyo: Abdominal Breathing.
Fukuto: Atemi Point just above the Knee.
Fumikomi Age uke: Rising Block Stepping In
Fumi Komi Geri: Stamping Kick
Fumikomi Shuto Uke: Knifehand Block Stepping In.
Fumikomi Ude Uke: Forearm Block Stepping In

Funakoshi Gichin: Founder of **Shotokan** Karate and Considered by Many to be the "Farther of Japanese Karate"
Futari Waza: Two Man Attacks

G

Gaiwan: Outer Edge of Arm.
Gaeshi: To Reverse
Ganmen: The Face
Ganseki Otoshi: Arm Bar with Elbow Brace Over Shoulder
Garami: To Entangle or Wrap
Garami Waza: Entangling Techniques
Gedan: Lower Level.
Gedan Barai: Sweeping Block
Gedan Choku Tsuke: Straight Punch to Groin.
Gedan Kake Uke: Downward Hooking Block.
Gedan Kekomi: Thrust Kick to Groin.
Gekon: Pressure Point to Lower Lip.
Gekyu: Low-level **Kyu,** the First Rank
Geri: Kick
Gi: Skill
Gi: Japanese Martial Art Uniform.
Gonosen-No-Kata; Judo, Kata of Counters
Go: Five
Godan: Fifth Dan. A Mid-High, Black Belt Rank.
Gokoku: Pressure Point in the Fleshy Area Between the Thumb and Forefinger.
Gyakon: Pressure Point on Lower Radial Nerve.
Gokyo: Aikido, Fifth Principle.
Goshi: Hip
Goshin Jutsu: Modern **Ju Jutsu** for Self Defence.
Gyaku: Reverse
Gyaku Geki: Counter Attack
Gyaku Juji Gamtame: Reverse Cross Arm Lock
Gyaku-Juji-Jime: Reverse Cross Strangle.
Gyaku kote gaeshi: Reverse Small Wrist Turn
Gyaku Tsuki: Reverse Punch

H

Ha: Tooth
Ha: Blade
Hachi: Eight
Hachi Dan: Eighth Dan
Hachimaki: Head Band
Hadaka: Nude, Bare
Hadaka Jime: Naked Neck Lock

Hai: Lungs (also Yes)
Haishu: Back Of the Hand
Haiwan: Back of the Forearm
Hajime: Start or Begin
Hakama: Divided Baggy Trouser worn while Practising Traditional Japanese Arts. They have Seven Pleats, Five at the Front and Two at the Back
Haito: Ridge Hand.
Haito Uchi: Ridge Hand Strike
Hanbo: 2-3 Foot staff.
Hanshi: Past-Master.
Hara: Stomach
Hara Kiri: Another term for **Seppuku** (ritual suicide.)
Harai: Sweeping
Harai Goshi: Sweeping Hip Throw.
Hariken or Hiraken: Fore-Knuckle Fist.
Hi: Spleen.
Hidari: Left
Hiji Ate: Elbow Strikes
Hima: Fore Head.
Hiza: Knee
Hiza Geri: Knee Kick
Hiza Garuma/Guruma: Knee Wheel.
Hombu: Head Office and Dojo.

I

I: Stomach
Iai: Sword Draw
Iaido: Modern Art of Swordsmanship.
Ichi: One
Ichiban: Number One, The Best
Idori: Techniques practised from **Seiza** (seated position)
Ifu: Dojo Tradition.
Ikkyo: Aikido Fist Principle
Ippon: Winning Point in **Judo** competition.
Ippon Ken: One Knuckle Fist.
Ippon Kumite: Practising Karate Movements using one Step.
Ippon Seio Nage: One arm Shoulder Throw.
Irimi: Entering
Irimi Nage: Enter Body Throw

J

Jigai: Japanese Women's Ritual Suicide Method.
Jin: Human/ Person.
Jintai: The Body.

Jin(zo): The Kidneys.
Jo: A Staff usually about 4 Feet Long.
Jo: Upper
Jo Jutsu: Stick Fighting Art
Jodan: Head Level.
Jodan Age Uke: Rising Block.
Jodan Tsuki: Upper Cut.
Jojutsu: The Art of using a Jo Staff.
Jonin: Ninja Leader.
Ju: Pliable, Ssupple and Yielding
Ju: Ten
Judo: The Gentle Way.
Judan: Tenth Dan
Ju Jutsu: Supple or Pliant Martial art. A Japanese Martial Art.
Juji: Cross.
Juji Gatame: Cross Arm Lock.
Juji Uke: Cross Block.
Ju-No-Kata: Judo Kata of Suppleness.
Jutsu: Art or Skill.
Jutte: Japanese weapon, Looks like half a Sai Dagger.

K

Kage Geri: Hooking Kick.
Kage Tsuki: Hooking Punch
Kaeshi-waza: Counter Techniques.
Kai: Association, Federation or Society.
Kaiken: A Short Dagger Carried by Women of the Bushi Class: Sometimes used to commit Ritual Suicide
Kaiten: To Spin, Turn or Spiral.
Kaiten Nage: Spiral Throw.
Ka-Jutsu: Fire or Explosive Techniques.
Kakato: Heel.
Kakato Geri: Heel Kick
Kama: A Smaller Version of Sickle.
Kamae: Posture.
Kan: House or Hall.
Kani Basami: Scissors Technique
Kano, Jigoro: Founder of **Kodokan** Judo.
Kansetsu Waza: Joint Manipulation Techniques.
Karate: Empty Hand
Kata: Shoulder
Kata: A Series of Martial Art Techniques to enhance the Art Practised.
Kata Guruma: Shoulder Wheel Throw.
Katame Waza: Grappling Techniques.
Katame No Kata: Kata of Ground Work Techniques.

Katana: Japanese Long Sword.
Katate: Single Hand.
Katate Yori: One Hand Holding other Persons Single Hand.
Katsu: The Art of Resuscitation also To Win, Be Victorious
Ke Age: Snap Kick.
Kekomi: Thrust kick.
Kempo: Iron Fist also known as Fist Law. Chinese Influenced Fighting Systems
Ken: Fist
Ken: Blade
Kendo: Modern Japanese Sporting Method using **Shinai** instead of Swords.
Kengo: Sword Master
Kenjutsu: Traditional Japanese Methods of using Swords.
Kenpo: See Kempo
Kenshutu: Swordsmanship.
Keppan: Blood Seal. A Vow or Oath Taken by a Student before being accepted into a Tradional School
Kesa Gatame: Scarf Hold
Ki: Inner Spirit or Strength.
Kiai: Unification of Energy: Usually Done by Means of a Loud Yell or Shout.
Kiai Jutsu: An Ancient Art that Concentrates on the Development and Accurate use of the Kiai
Kiba Dachi: Straddle Stance.
Kihon: Basics.
Kihon Kumite: Basic Sparring.
Kime No Kata: Kata of Self-defence.
Kin Geri: Groin Kick.
Ko: Minor.
Kodokan: The World Judo Headquarters Located in Tokyo
Kokyu: Breathing.
Koroshi: Death Blow.
Koppo Jutsu: Bone Breaking Techniques.
Ko Soto Gari: Minor Outer Reaping Throw.
Ko Shi: Ball of Foot.
Koshiki No Kata: Ancient Kata from **Judo**.
Kote Gaeshi: Small Wrist Turn.
Ko Uchi Gari: Minor Inner Reaping Throw.
Ku: Nine.
Kubi: Neck.
Kubu Nage: Neck Throw
Kuchi: Mouth.
Kuchibiru: Lips.
Kuzushi: To Break the Opponents Balance
Kyu: Boy
Kyu: Name Given to Grading System Building up to Black Belt.
Kyudo: Modern art of Japanese archery.

Kyu Jutsu: Classical Japanese Art Of archery.

M

Ma: Distance
Maai: Combat Engagement Distance
Mae: Front or Forward
Mae Geri: Front Kick
Mae Tobi Geri: Jumping Front Kick
Mae Ukemi: Front Breakfall
Maki: Wrapped around
Makikomi: Winding
Makiwara: Striking Board for Conditioning the Hands
Manriki Gusari: Chained Weapon with Weight on One or Both Ends
Matte: Stop
Mawashi: A Rotational Turn
Mawashi Geri: Round House Kick
Mawashi Tsuke: Round House Punch
Mawatte: Turn Around
Me: Eyes
Meijin: Someone who h\as Achieved Mental, Spiritual, and Physical Perfection in their Art
Men: Head, Face
Migi: Right
Migi Suki Geri: Crescent Kick
Mimi: Ears
Momo: Thigh
Mon: Japanese Crest
Morote: Using both Hands
Morote Gyaku Soto Uke: Reinforced Reversed Outside Forearm Block
Morote Gyaku Tsuki: Reinforced Reverse Punch
Morote Jodan Age Uke: Reinforced Rising Block
Morote Koken Uchi: Reinforced Arc Fist Strike
Morote Nukite Uchi: Reinforced Straight Finger Strike
Morote Shuto Uchi: Reinforced Knife Edge Hand Strike
Morote Sote Uke: Reinforced Outside Forearm Block
Mune: Chest
Mushin: State of Mind when Facing an Opponent. The Mind should be Clear of Thought

N

Nagashi: Flowing
Nagashi Waza: Flowing Techniques
Nage: Throw
Nage Waza: Throwing Technique
Naginata: Polearm Weapon with Long Shaft and Curved Blade
Naifu: Knife

Naka: Centre or Middle
Nakadaka: Middle Knuckle
Nami Jiji Jime: Normal Cross Strangle
Neko Ashi Dachi: Cat Stance
Ni: Two
Nidan: Second Dan
Nihon also Nippon: The correct Name for Japan
Nihon Nukite: Two Finger strike
Nikkyo: Aikido Second Principle
Ninja: Japanese Assassin, Spy
Ninja-To: Ninja Sword, Straight Blade
Ninjutsu: The Art of Stealth
Ninpo: The **Ninja** Way
Nodo: Throat
Nukite: Straight Fingers Spear Hand
Nunchaku: Rice Flail, Two Sticks made from various materials attached by a cord or chain

O

O: Great, Major
O Goshi: Major Hip Throw
O Guruma: major Wheel
O Soto Gari: Major Outer Reaping Throw
O Uchi Gari: Major Inner Reaping Throw
Obi: Belt
Obi Otoshi: Belt Lifting Drop
Okuden: Secret Techniques
Okuri Eri Jime: Sliding Collar Neck Lock
Osae: Immobilize
Osae Komi: Called in Judo Competitions to Recognize a Hold Down
Osae Waza: Immobilization Techniques
O Sensei: Great Teacher

P

Pinan: A Group of Five Basic Okinawan Kata's

R

Randori: Free Style Sparring
Rei: Bow
Reigi: Etiquette
Renshu: Hard Work
Renzoku: Geri: Combination Techniques
Ritsu Rei: Standing Bow
Roku: Six
Rokodan: Sixth Dan

Ronin: Samurai Warrior. With no Lord
Ryote Dori: Holding Both Hands
Ryu: An Art, Style

S

Sabaki: Body Motion
Sai: A Steel Trident
Samurai: Ancient Japanese Warrior. One Who Serves
San: Three
Sanchin Dachi: Hour Glass Stance
Sandan: Third Dan
Sankyo: Aikido Third Principle
Saya: Scabbard
Seika Tanden: Lower Abdomen. The Seat of Energy Based Three Inches Below the Navel
Seiken: Forefist
Seiken Tsuke: Forefist Strike
Seikichu: The Spine
Seionage: Shoulder Throw
Semban Nage: Shuriken Throwing Techniques
Sempai: Senior Student
Sen: The Number 1000
Senaka: The Back of the Body
Senjutsu: Tactics
Sensei: Teacher or Instructor
Sensei Ni Rei: Bow to the Teacher
Seppuka: Japanese Ritual Suicide
Shi: Four
Shiatsu: Tem for Japanese Acupressure Massage
Shichi: Seven
Shihan: A Senior Instructor
Shiho: Four Directions
Shiho Nage: Four Direction Throw
Shin: Heart
Shinai: Bamboo Sword used in **Kendo**
Shintai: The Body
Shomen: Face, Front Head
Shomen Uchi: Downward Blow
Shougun: General
Shuriken: Throwing Stars
Shuto: Knife Edge Hand
Shuto Uchi: Knife Edge Hand Strike
Shuto Uke: Knife Edge Hand Block
Sode: Sleeve
Sode Dori: Sleeve Grab
Sode Tsuri Komi Goshi: Sleeve Lift Pull Hip Throw

Soji: The Cleaning of the **Dojo**
Sojutsu: Spear Art
Soke: Head of Family and Head of Style
Sokei: Groin
Sokuso: Tips of the Toes
Sokutei: Bottom of the Heel
Sokuto: Edge of the Foot
Sokuto Yoko Geri: Side Kick Using the Edge of the Foot
Soto: Outer, Outside
Soto Uke: Outside Forearm Block
Suigetsu: Solar Plexus
Sukui: Scooping
Sukui Uke: Scooping Block
Sumi Gaeshi: Corner Throw
Sutemi Waza: Sacrifice Throw
Suwatte: Sit Down

T

Tabi: Shoes and Socks Divided by the Big Toe
Tachi: Standing
Tachi: Battle Sword longer than a **Katana**
Tachi Waza: Standing Techniques
Tai: Body
Tai Jutsu: Body Art, Skill. Old **Ju-Jutsu** System
Tai Otoshi: Body Drop
Taisabaki: Evasive Body Movement Using Circular Movement with the Feet
Tameshiwari: Showing Skill and Power by Demonstrating Breaking Techniques
Tan: Gallbladder
Tanden: Abdomen
Tani: Valley
Tani Otoshi: Valley Drop
Tanko: Bladder
Tanto: Knife with a blade between 4" and 13" The Knife used in Ritual Suicide
Tanto Jutsu: knife Fighting Skills
Tatami: Mat Area
Tate Shiho Gatame: Vertical four Quarters Hold
Tawara Geashi: Bale Throw
Teisho: Palm Heel on the Hand
Teisho Uke: Palm heel Block
Tem Ben Nage: Elbow Lock Throw
Tenchi: Heaven and Earth
Tenchi Nage: Heaven and Earth Throw
Tenkan: The Opposite to **Irimi**. To Go to the Outside
Tettsui: Hammer Fist
Te Waza: Hand Techniques

Tobi: Jump
Tobi Geri: Jumping Kick
Token Jutsu: Blade Throwing Techniques
Tonfa: Wood Staff with a Handle on the Side
Tori: Defender
Tsuki: punch
Tsuke Waza: Punching Techniques

U

Uchi: Strike
Uchi Waza: Striking techniques
Ude: The Arm. Inside
Ude Garame: Entangled Arm Lock
Ude Gatame: Arm lock with Hands
Ude Uke: Inside Forearm Block
Uke: Attacker
Ukemi: Breakfalls
Uki: Floating
Uki Goshi: Floating Hip Throw
Ura: Back
Ura Nage: Back Throw
Uraken: Back of the Fist
Uraken Uchi: Backfist Strike
Ushiro: Rear, Behind
Ushiro Geri: Back Kick
Uwagi: Uniform Jacket

W

Wake Gatami: Elbow Lock
Waki: Side: Armpit
Wan: Arm
Wanto: Arm Sword
Wakizashi: A Short Sword Carried as a Companion to the **Katana**
Waza: Technique

Y

Yama: Mountain
Yame: Stop
Yari: Spear
Yari Jutsu: Spear Throwing Techniques
Yoi: Ready
Yoko: To the Side
Yoko Geri: Side Kick
Yoko Guruma: Side Wheel Throw

Yoko Uchi: A Side Strike
Yoko Ukemi: Side Breakfall
Yokomen: Side of the Head
Yokomen Uchi: A Blow to the Side of the Head
Yonkyo: Aikido Fourth Principle
Yoroi: Armor
Toroi Nage: Armor Throws
Yowai: Weak
Yowaki: Weak Energy
Yubi: Finger
Yudansha: Black Belt Level
Yuki: Courage
Yukuri: Slow
Yumi: A Bow as used in **Kyudo**

Z

Za: Sitting
Za Rei: Kneeling Salutation (Bow)
Zanshin: State of Awareness
Zekken: Badge with ones own name or the Dojo Name on it
Zen: Philosophy and a Religion
Zenkutsu Dachi: Forward Stance
Zori: Japanese Sandals for use off the **Tatami** in the Dojo
Zubon: Trousers

Martial Arts Ranks

Because of all the different styles of martial arts around today, the colour of the Kyu grade belts vary so much that it is difficult to document. So where did coloured belts come from?

Well it all started about 1605. The Tokugawa court of Japan patronizes the Go Academy, of a master called Honinbo Sansha. This introduces Haninbo's method of classifying students, e.g. shodan for the first dan, nidan for the second dan, and so on. To the Samurai class.

1883. Kano Jigoro decided to divide his students into two separate groups, ungraded (mudansha) and graded (yudansha). The first students to achieve graded rank (shodan 1st Dan) were Tomita Tsunejiro and Saigo Shiro. Around 1886 or 1887, Kano's ungraded students began wearing white belts while his graded students began to wearing black belts.

From this time on the belt system was borne and every martial art and style now has it own colour system.

Pre Black Belt Ranks

10th Kyu	Jukyu
9th Kyu	Kukyu
8th Kyu	Hachikyu
7th Kyu	Sichikyu
My Kempo Karate Starts Here 6th Kyu White belt	Rokkyu
5th Kyu Yellow belt	Rokkyu
4th Kyu Orange belt	Yonkyu
3rd Kyu Green belt	Sankyu
2nd Kyu Blue belt	Nikyu
1st Kyu Brown belt	Ikkyu

Black Belt Ranks

1st Dan	Shodan
2nd Dan	Nidan
3rd Dan	Sandan
4th Dan	Yondan

5th Dan	Godan
6th Dan	Rokudan
7th Dan	Sichidan
8th Dan	Hachidan
9th Dan	Kudan
10th Dan	Judan

Japanese Numbers 1 through 20

1	Ichi
2	Ni
3	San
4	Shi
5	Go
6	Roku
7	Shichi
8	Hachi
9	Ku
10	Ju
11	Juichi
12	Juni
13	Jusan
14	Jugo
15	Jugo
16	Juroku
17	Jushichi
18	Juhachi
19	Juku
20	Niju

Karate Syllabus

White Belt 6th Kyu
BLOCKS

JODAN AGE UKE	RISING BLOCK
GEDAN BARAI	DOWNWARD BLOCK
UDE UKE	INSIDE FOREARM BLOCK
SOTO UKE	OUTSIDE FOREARM BLOCK

BLOCK SEQUENCE
STANCES

ZENKUTSU DACHI	FRONT STANCE
JU DACHI	FREE STYLE STANCE
KIBA DACHI	STRADDLE STANCE

HAND TECHNIQUES

OIE TSUKI	LUNGE PUNCH
GYAKU TSUKI	REVERSE PUNCH

KICKS

MAE GERI	FRONT KICK
YOKO GERI	SIDE KICK
MAWASHI GERI	ROUND HOUSE KICK
USHIRO GERI	BACK KICK

BREAKFALLS

YOKO UKEMI	SIDE BREAKFALL
USHIRO UKEMI	BACK BREAKFALL

Plus: defences from attacks to the head, attack to be downward blows, side blows, punches to the face
Plus: defence form front and rear bear hugs (with and without arms pinned).
Plus: defences from front and rear strangulation's
Plus: defences from front and rear hair pulls.

Note all movement to be practiced right and left

5th Kyu Yellow Belt

BLOCKS

JODAN JUJI UKE	RISING CROSS BLOCK
GEDAN JUJI UKE	DOWNWEARD CROSS BLOCK
STUTO UKE	KNIFE HAND BLOCK
TEISHO UKE	PALM HEEL BLOCK

Blocks must be demonstrated in various stances

STANCES

KO KUTSU DACHI	BACK STANCE
NEKO ASHI DACHI	CAT STANCE

Combinations of stances e.g Kokutsu Dachi, Zenkutsu Dachi

HAND TECHNIQUES

SHUTO UCHI	KNIFE HAND ATTACK
URAKEN UCHI	BACK FIST ATTACK
TETSUI UCHI	HAMMER FIST ATTACK

KICKS

MAE GERI	KICK OF FRONT LEG
YOKO GERI	CLOSE QUARTER SIDE KICK
MAWASHI GERI	KICK OF FRONT LEG
USHIRO MAWASHI GERI	REVERSE ROUND HOUSE KICK

Kicks to be done from various stances

ROLLS AND BREAKFALLS

JEMPO KAITEN	FORWARD ROLL
USHIRO KAITEN	BACKWARD ROLL
MAA UKEMI	FRONT BREAKFALL

Plus: defences from lapels held one and two hands
Plus: defences from lapel held with blow to the head they will be , side blow, downward blow and straight punch
Plus: defences from both hands being restrained from the rear
Plus defences from the attacker pulling your shoulder from the rear with and without a blow
Plus: defences from the attacker pulling your sleeve from the rear with and without a blow

3rd Kyu Orange Belt

BLOCKS

KOKEN UKE	ARC FIST BLOCK
TEISHO UKE	PALM HEEL BLOCK
EMPI UKE	ELBOW BLOCK

Combination of blocks (random)

HAND TECHNIQUES

JODAN TSUKI	UPPER CUT
MAWASHI TSUKI	ROUND HOUSE PUNCH
HAITO UKE	RIDGE HAND STRIKE

Stances; all previous plus to demonstrate stances incorporating Kicks Strikes and Blocks

KICKS

MIGI SUKI GERI	CRESENT KICK (FRONT AND BACK LEG)
USHIRO MIGI SUKI GERI	REVERSE CRESENT KICK (FRONT AND BACK LEG)
MIGI SUKI GERI	JUMPING VERSION
MIGI SUKI GERI	REVERSE JUMPING VERSION

BREAKFALLS AND ROLLS

MAA UKEMI	FRONT BREALFALL TO STAGE 3
JEMPO KAITEN TO YOKO UKIMI	FORWARD ROLL TO SIDE BREAKFALL

Plus: defences from kicks, front kick, side kick, round house kick, back kick. Defence will be done from low, midrange and high kicks.
Plus: defences from strangulation's whilst being pinned against a wall
Plus: defence from side head locks with and without a blow to the face
Plus: defence from forearm nelson
Plus: defences from kicks whilst you are on the floor on your back.

3rd Kyu Green Belt

BLOCKS

SUKI UKE	SCOOPING BLOCK (OUTSIDE AND INSIDE)
TEISHO UKE	PALM HEEL BLOCK

HAND TECHNIQUES

NUKITE UCHI	STRAIGHT FINGER STRIKE
TOHO UCHI	SWORD HILT STRIKE
IPPON NUKITE	ONE FINGER STRIKE
NIHON NUKITE	TWO FINGER STRIKE

KICKS

SPIP IN FRONT KICK
SKIP IN SIDE KICK
SKIP IN ROUND HOUSE KICK
STEP BACK, BACK KICK
REVERSE JUMP FRONT KICK
STEP UP ON BOX AND JUMP FRONT KICK
JUMPING SIDE KICK
JUMPING ROUND HOUSE KICK

BREAKFALLS

FOUR POINT LANDING (THREE STAGES)

Plus Defences from cosh. Attack's to be; Downward and side blows and reverse hand attack.
Plus Defences from two man attack. Attacks to be; hands restrained, arms restrained and one holding from the rear and the other attacking.
Plus 2 minutes sparring.

2nd Kyu Blue Belt

BLOCKS

MOROTE JODAN AGE UKI	RIENFORCED RISING BLOCK
MOROTE SOTE UKI	RIENFORCED OUTSIDE FOREARM BLOCK
MOROTE GYAKU SOTE UKI	RIENFORCED REVERSE OUTSIDE FOREARM BLOCK
MOROTE UDE UKE	RIENFORCED INSIDE FOREARM BLOCK

HAND TECHNIQUES

MOROTE OIE TSUKI	RIENFORCED LUNGE PUNCH
MOROTE GYAKU TSUKI	RIENFORCED REVERSE PUNCH
MOROTE KOKEN UCHI	RIENFORCE ACR FIST STRIKE
MOROTE SHUTO UCHI	REINFORCE KNIFE ENDGE HAND
MOROTE NUKITE UCHI	REINFORCE STRAIGHT FINGER STRIKE

KICKS, COMBINATIONS

FRONT TO SIDE KICK	SIDE KICK TO ROUND HOUSE KICK
FRONT ANGLED KICK TO ROUND HOUSE KICK	FRONT KICK TO BACK KICK
FOUR KICK COMBINATION x 2	

Defences
Ten defences against cosh
Six defences against knife attacks
Four defences against gun
Ten immobilization techniques
Defences from three man attack's
Breaking techniques, own choice
Sparring with knockdowns

1st Kyu Brown Belt

BLOCKS

DOUBLE BLOCKS, VARIOUS COMBINATIONS

HAND TECHNIQUES

DOUBLE HAND TECHNIQUES, VARIOUS COMBINATIONS

KICKS

FLOOR FRONT KICK	BALL, TOP, HEEL, AXE, FRONT ANGLED.
FLOOR SIDE KICK	HEEL, BALL, EDGE.
FLOOR ROUND HOUSE KICK	SHIN, BALL, TOP.
FLOOR BACK KICK	HEEL
FLOOR CRESCENT KICK	
FLOOR REVERSE CRESENT KICK	

Kata
Develop own kata, 32 moves

Ten combination techniques
Ten counter techniques
Ten knife techniques
Ten gun techniques
Ten cosh techniques
Fifteen immobilization techniques
Fifty atemi waza's
Breaking techniques, own choice
Sparring
Line up or circle attacks

James Moclair

Black Belt, 1st Dan

BLOCKS AND HAND COMBINATIONS

RISING BLOCK PLUS	REVERSE PUNCH
INSIDE FOREARM BLOCK PLUS	RIDGE HAND STRIKE
REVERSE OUTSIDE FOREARM BLOCK PLUS	KNIFE HAND STRIKE
OUTSIDE FOREARM BLOCK PLUS	TWIST PUNCH
RANDOM MOVEMENTS	

KICKS

VARIOUS HOOK KICKS	
VARIOUS TWIST KICKS	
VARIOUS KNEE KICKS	
VARIOUS SHIN KICKS	
REACTION WORK ON PADS +	HAND AND FOOT

Kata
Develop own kata, 52 moves

Twenty combination techniques
Twenty counter techniques
Twenty knife techniques
Fifteen gun techniques
Twenty cosh techniques
Twenty immobilization techniques
One hundred atemi waza's
Breaking techniques, own choice
Sparring
Line up or circle attacks
A good sound knowledge of first aid
Teaching ability.

With Thanks

Thanks everyone

I would not have been able to complete this book without the help from the following person's.

Lee is student and friend of mine, at the time of writing this book he was only eighteen years old, but he has helped me overcome so many technical obstacles that without his computer and photographic skills and "wise old head" I would not have achieved anything like what I have done with out Lee's help. Thanks Lee.

Dan is Lee's brother, and I would like thank Dan for his time and assistance. Dan is the one in the photos with the socks on. Many thanks Dan.

At the start of the white belt and yellow belt attacks and defences, you can see some incredible photographic posses. This is my good friend and student Rob, he really put a lot into his role. Thanks for all your help Rob.

Although Lee took a large amount of the photos in the book, my good friend Tal did an excellent job also. Thanks Tal.

And from time to time I had to take the photo's on auto timer, with me running from the camera to the pose position, so thanks to the person who developed the auto timer.

About the Author

James Moclair is a Professor of BuJutsu, (Japanese martial arts). He is a professional martial arts teacher and had been doing martial arts for forty two years. James has an impressive career that has taken him around the world and has even been World Champion and Gold medallist representing England.

James's current martial arts grades are, 10th Dan Ju-jutsu and this relates to four different styles of Ju-jutsu, 8th Dan Karate, 8th Dan Ko-Budo, 6th Dan Aiki-jutsu, 5th Dan Judo, Ki master. This indeed is an outstanding achievement and has only come about by years of dedication and hard work.

What is even more impressive that James spends over seventy six hours a week at his Dojo, (martial arts centre) where he teaches and keeps up his own training. And if you think that is impressive let me tell you that he also does this seven days a week.

When James is relaxing he likes to play video games and his favourites are the martial beat up games. He also likes to read a good book and has read several hundreds of books.

http://www.taijutsukwai.com